D0421830

Friends, Moments, Countryside

Friends, Moments, Countryside

Selected Columns from Canadian Living, 1993-98

PETER GZOWSKI

Canadian Cataloguing in Publication Data

Gzowski, Peter
Friends, moments, countryside : selected columns
from Canadian living, 1993-98

Includes bibliographical references.
ISBN 0-7710-3699-X

I. Title. II. Title: Canadian living.

PS8563.Z69F74 1998 C814′.54 C98-931260-7
PR9199.3.G96F74 1998

We acknowledge the financial support of the Government of Canada through the Book Publishing Industry Development Program for our publishing activities. We further acknowledge the support of the Canada Council for the Arts and the Ontario Arts Council for our publishing program.

Set in Bembo by M&S, Toronto
Printed and bound in Canada

McClelland & Stewart Inc.
The Canadian Publishers
481 University Avenue
Toronto, Ontario
M5G 2E9

1 2 3 4 5 02 01 00 99 98

Table of Contents

Introduction

Part One: Friends

Part Two: Moments

Part Three: Countryside

INTRODUCTION

As Canadian as Possible . . .

INTRODUCTION

As Canadian as Possible . . .

NEARLY ALL THE COLUMNS in this collection, which ran in *Canadian Living* magazine between 1993 and 1998, were written in the place I have tried to describe here in the piece called "Home" (there was, as there were for most of these pieces, a slightly different title in the magazine), and nearly all were written on weekends. Oh, there were exceptions. Sometimes I wrote at Swallow Point, the enchanted house in Nova Scotia that also makes an appearance here, where I scribbled away on one of the spacious sun porches, east by morning, west in the gentle afternoons, and later, drove my handwritten manuscript into downtown Chester to scrounge a word processor and a fax. And sometimes I wrote on what broadcasters, unfortunately, call "the road" (more often than not, it simply means outside Toronto); I remember, for example, working something up in a hotel in Rankin Inlet and riding a snowmobile out to my friend Michael Kusugak's writing shack on the shore of Hudson's Bay, where, among the sealskins and the narwhal tusks, I borrowed some of the most sophisticated electronic communications devices I've ever encountered. The month after that, I was in Bermuda — on holiday this time — chuckling over Robin Skelton's recipe for celery sticks in a folder full of recipes, and trying to catch the flavour of the Sechelt Writers Conference on the Sunshine Coast of B.C. But mostly, even when I was remembering other places — Watson Lake in the Yukon, White Rock, Wolfville (a column that resulted in my hearing from what I'm pretty sure was every real estate agent in the Annapolis Valley), or Galt, the small city in southwestern Ontario where I grew up — I was at Lake Simcoe. I wrote in the airy study my cousin Jack built for me, with a fire crackling in the hearth or the summer sun beaming on the garden outside my window, and if some of the peace and contentment I feel in that refuge shows through here, well, that's often what I was writing about, isn't it?

IN THE PUBLIC ARENA, THESE were turbulent times for Canada. Only eight years after having rung up the largest majority in parliamentary history, and having begun dramatically and perhaps irreversibly to reshape the country, the Mulroney Conservatives — technically the Kim Campbell Conservatives by then but still Mulroneyites in the public mind — were swept away in an unparalleled tide of revulsion. The Chrétien Liberals, after a vigorous and high minded campaign against such Tory innovations as free trade and the GST, picked up precisely where their hated predecessors had left off, and in many ways outdid them; if anything, the reshaping accelerated. The fledgling Reform Party, whose roots in the West's discontent were still not understood by Eastern élites (although the Liberals cagily usurped much of Reform's platform, just as their forebears had incorporated many of the ideas of the CCF and the NDP), entrenched its beachhead in the west, and emerged, after one false start, as Her Majesty's Opposition, complete with a freshly recoiffed leader who surmounted his fears of being corrupted and moved into the leader's comfortable official residence at Stornaway. Only in Ontario, where Reform had hoped to expand its geographical base, did the wave of Western populist protest run aground, yet Ontario voters, at their first opportunity, put into office a premier who on many fronts out Reformed the forces of Preston Manning.

Quebec, not uncharacteristically, was the most volatile of all the provinces. Réné Lévesque was gone, and after the grace with which he had taken his defeat in the first referendum and his subsequent untimely death, the movement he had led had seemed to lose its momentum. Quebeckers had turned from nationalist politics to commerce, building what became known as Quebec Inc., and finding in its structure the economic autonomy they had so long been denied. Robert Bourassa, the wily and sometimes Machiavellian technocrat — but a federalist nonetheless* — had come to power. But then came Meech Lake and its failure. Sensing a new mood and a chance to put his mark on constitutional history, Brian Mulroney had called the premiers together and hammered out an agreement that, whatever its other shortcomings, would give Quebec its place in Confederation's sun. When that agreement foundered, notably in the legislatures of Manitoba and Newfoundland, and despite the fact that much of the opposition in the rest of the country was based on other reasons, Quebec felt rejected. More than rejected —

---

* I interviewed Bourassa a number of times over these years, most often in the imposing Quebec City eyrie the press corps call "the Bunker." It was always a fascinating experience, though sometimes frustrating. Once, just before I was going to meet him, I asked Morningside's widely respected trio of political pundits — the three wise men, as we called them — what they'd ask him if they had the chance. "Simple," said the redoubtable Eric Kierans. "Ask him if he's a Canadian." I did, and got my answer: yes. But it was phrased without enthusiasm, and couched in typical Bourassan obfuscation. Later, I complained of this privately to Frank McKenna, who had become good friends with his Quebec counterpart. "You don't understand," McKenna said. "He can't say what you'd like him to say. Every word he utters is watched by *Le Devoir*. Ask him first about economics, which he's comfortable talking about. Then get into his commitment to federalism. It's real, but he has to be careful."

hurt and insulted.* The flames of nationalism leaped back to life, fanned this time not by the likable former war correspondent Lévesque, whose countenance, in black and white, still dominates a subterranean hallway in the Radio Canada building on the Montreal boulevard that now bears his name, but by the standoffish, single-minded and distinctly *un*likable economist Jacques Parizeau, who had, when they were colleagues, thought Lévesque too patient.

To Ottawa, the voters sent a curious assortment of union leaders, academics and small-business people, united only by their conviction that the parliament in which they served enacted laws for a country that was not their own. There were, however, enough of them that for one term, until Reform edged them out, they formed what their critics in English-speaking Canada liked to remind them with sour irony was still presumed to be Her Majesty's "Loyal" Opposition. Their leader, Lucien Bouchard, was despised by English-speaking Canadians as a turncoat and a liar, demonized by everyone from the Reform Party to the brilliant comedians of This Hour Has 22 Minutes — although, perhaps typically, the whole of the country responded with sympathy

* I remember sitting on a plane with a friend from the literacy movement, a senior and bilingual Ottawa civil servant who had worked hard behind the scenes for Meech Lake's acceptance. "My own eighty-year-old mother," he said, "took it personally. After all these years, she's become a separatist. That's how deep these feelings go."

when mysterious flesh-eating bacteria threatened his life. But for the sovereigntists of Quebec, he was the saviour incarnate. When Parizeau left office in bitterness and frustration after his heart-stoppingly close loss in the second referendum and his unfortunate voting-night remark about "money and the ethnic vote"—the only occasion most of us could remember when a politician, however much his vision may have been lubricated by Scotch whisky, was vilified for having spoken what was, after all, the truth—it was Bouchard, the former Mulroney cabinet minister and Canadian ambassador to France, who was summoned from Ottawa to replace him.

Bouchard's charismatic popularity, still underestimated by federalists outside his native province, continued unabashed, and the clock seemed to be ticking toward yet another referendum. When Daniel Johnson, the stout-hearted but uninspiring leader of the provincial Liberals, stepped sadly down from his office in the winter of '98, Jean Charest, one of the few white knights of the last close call, but a reluctant standard-bearer, rode out of the West—and his own Mulroneyite past—to take up the challenge. Many federalist hearts were lifted. But those who knew Quebec knew that to have any chance of ousting the forces of evil, Charest would have to espouse the legitimate aspirations of the nationalists. Not as the sovereigntists had, perhaps, and certainly not with an eye to yet another referendum, which the voters clearly did not want. But however committed Charest was to Canada, he was also determined to strengthen Quebec's place in it, and it was that desire that would, by political necessity if nothing else, be a central theme of his message as Liberal leader — or even, as federalists dared to hope, as premier. Quebec's dissatisfaction with the *status quo* was far from over.

At the same time, there was, or seemed to be, a hardening of resistance in English-speaking Canada.* Enough is enough, people were saying; no matter how many concessions we make they want more. This attitude troubled many federalists, who felt that most of what Quebec had achieved and was still after would have no measurable effect on people's real, day-to-day lives. But, fanned by the Reform Party (among others), it helped give rise to the federal government's curiously named Plan B: a tough-love approach that would spell out the ramifications of a separatist vote and which led to the Supreme Court reference on the legality of a unilateral declaration, and which seemed, to its opponents at least, to run the risk of being self-fulfilling.

Constitutional wrangles aside — and even in Quebec there was a weariness with the endless bickering — the real story of Canadian politics in the years these columns were written was the national swing to what was all too easily called the right. The days of lavish spending in the public sector were over, as governments at every level resolved to

---

* Sometimes, for those of us who thought it important to use this term — a reminder that Canada outside francophone Quebec was a mosaic of many racial textures — the task was difficult. I remember in particular daring to correct, in a Morningside interview, none other than Lucien Bouchard, who, to his credit, pondered for a moment, then conceded that it was more accurate than simple "English Canada."

chop their deficits and even head towards making some inroads into their monstrous debts. Provincially, the leaders of this crusade were perceived to be, first, Ralph Klein in Alberta and, later but even more dramatically (and without Klein's energy-based bonanza to help him), Mike Harris in Ontario. But premiers of all political labels were in the race; the first balanced budget, in fact, was brought down not by one of the slash-and-burn Tories, or even the businesslike (and immensely popular) Liberal Frank McKenna in New Brunswick, but by Roy Romanow, the heir to Tommy Douglas's social democratic legacy in Saskatchewan.

Nowhere was the drive to shrink the public sector more forceful than in Ottawa. As Tom Flanagan, the Calgary academic who was one of the founders of the Reform Party but who had left because he thought Preston Manning had gone soft on its economic agenda, said on a CBC Radio panel, "We've been able to get much more from Paul Martin than we ever got from Mulroney." Under Martin's leadership, with the proudly pragmatic Jean Chrétien cheering him on, program after program was cut, dispatched to the private sector, or dismantled. The railways, the harbours, air traffic control, support for the arts, scientific research, public broadcasting, the armed services, regional subsidies — many of the programs that had helped to define Canada — all felt the cold steel of Martin's knife. On health care, the single institution that Canadians felt most strongly about, the attack by the federal Liberals was not direct, but transfer payments to the provinces were so reduced that the cuts, some of them Draconian, came about anyway.

Many of these changes were unavoidable. Even those of us who worked in some of the public fields that were being shrunk — in my own case, the CBC — recognized the need for trimming and realized that there was a large measure of truth in the corporate leadership's argument that the rest of the prosperous world looked on us as spendthrifts, and that we had to trim our sails to compete in what we were constantly reminded was a new global economy. Well, sure, said a lot of people.* What concerned us was not the cuts themselves, but their degree and their urgency — and, at the core, the fact that many of them were imposed far more on the most vulnerable segments of society than on the élites that were driving them. The more we marched into what the media told us was prosperity — some of it, inarguably, brought about by North American free trade, which most of the left had opposed — the more we widened the gap between the powerful and the dispossessed. Canadian banks were making billion-dollar profits; Canadian children, in appalling numbers, were going hungry. The stock market zoomed ever upward; food banks strained to meet the demand. For every new millionaire there seemed to be at least one squeegee kid to wash his windows for loose change.

Canada still had universal medicare, despite increasing pressure to open the door to private-sector alternatives and

---

* Phrases such as "a lot of people" or "many of us" often really mean no more than the writer and some of his or her friends. This may well be the case here. But a lot of people did agree.

siphon off the wealthy into a comfortable tier of their own. And everyone agreed we had to look at changes — especially to incorporate more preventive medicine and more home care, which many health-care professionals had been advocating for years. But the system hadn't had *time* to change, just as it hadn't been ready for the flood of tranquillized humanity that poured into the back streets and tawdry rooming houses as pharmaceuticals replaced wards in the cuckoos' nests. In the throes of accommodation, fissures appeared everywhere. One of the more sombre stories of 1998 was about emergency wards in major cities having to turn patients away at the door. It was, if there ever was one, not a good time to be sick.

The stress on the health-care system was just one of the eddies in an inexorable tide: the Americanization of practically everything. For a long time, people who had wanted to delineate the differences between Canada and the United States had pointed to the fact that in Canada there was no national party far enough to the right to oppose universal medicare, while in the U.S. no party stood far enough to the left to favour it. There was, in other words, a different political centre of gravity. In the nineties, our system was not yet under formal attack by any of our major parties, and even the Clinton-led Democrats had not made universality part of their platform in the U.S.— there were still forty million Americans without health insurance. The observation about the political centre of gravity may still, indeed, have been true; as John R. McArthur, the publisher of *Harper's* magazine, pointed out in an article in the *Globe and Mail*, "Jean Chrétien's centrist policies would have made him unelectable to any [American] political office outside of Minnesota or the Upper West Side of Manhattan." But things were changing. The more we weakened our system of universal health care, the more the Americans thought about emulating it. If Canada had been a place where it was not quite so comfortable to be rich as in the United States, but a little less soul-destroying to be poor — and our attitude to health care was an expression of that feeling — then that difference, such as it was, was shrinking all the time.

So were others. Our Charter of Rights and Freedoms, proudly proclaimed in 1982, had, in spite of its curious and somehow typically Canadian "notwithstanding clause," contained at least two Americanizing notions, and through the years I was writing these columns those ideas continued to take root. One was simply the new powers the Charter gave to our courts, not only to interpret laws and rule on their admissibility as they were written, but at times actually to add to what Parliament had decreed. The widely discussed Vriend decision of 1998, in which the Supreme Court "read in" the rights of gays and lesbians to Alberta's human rights legislation, was a case in point. As well, the Charter tilted our law away from collective rights towards those of the individual. In many ways, those changes had been progress, for not even the most fervent of nationalists would argue that all American ideas are inferior to all Canadian principles. And for women, first nations, for many gays and lesbians — once again the Vriend decision was a case in point — and others, it was a step forward. But it was also a step towards the American way of justice. The balance between the rights of the individual and the rights of the community is a central debate of every civil society, and Canada is no exception. But in our case, collectivism —"huddling together against the cold"— had been a part of who we were. It underlay everything from our social safety network to our commitment to public broadcasting; if the private sector couldn't or wouldn't do it, we had always just banded together and done it publicly. The Charter didn't *expunge* this principle. But it modified it. It was another eddy in the tide.

Culturally, there were two mutually contradictory trends. On the one hand, some modes of our self-expression flowered. Canadian writing simply took off, continuing the revolution that had begun as long ago as the 1960s. Our writers not only brought our voices and our stories to our own best-seller lists, they carried them around the world. Nearly all this writing was in English (although there were such notable French achievements as the Prix Goncourt won by the Acadienne Antonine Maillet), but as never before its voices reflected the nation's diversity. Ondaatje, Bisoondath, Mistry, Vasanji, Mukharjee, Selvadorai, Kogawa, Choy, Lau, Chong, Ricci, Skvorecky — not to mention Tomson Highway, Thomas King, Don Ross and others of aboriginal descent — joined the ranks of Davies, Atwood, Laurence, Munro (widely regarded as the best short-story writer in the English language), Findley, Urquhart, Shields, Richler and Mitchell as authors of international esteem. In popular music, too, we continued to make our mark. At one point, four of the six most successful female vocalists in America — Celine Dion, Alanis Morrisette, Jann Arden and Shania Twain — were Canadian, with such other luminaries as Gordon Lightfoot, David Foster, Bryan Adams, Robbie Robertson, the Crash Test Dummies and Barenaked Ladies (we're good at naming groups, eh?) and the perennially popular Anne Murray also selling in the millions.

On other cultural fronts we were not so successful in stemming the tide. Canadian movies continued to struggle for exposure on Canadian screens, controlled, as those screens were, by international (read American) companies which viewed the Canadian audience as nothing more than an extension of the American market. Even our most acclaimed works — the oeuvre of the director Atom Egoyan was a dramatic example in 1998 — were swamped by promotional campaigns whose hoopla knew no borders. Canadian plays found themselves having to fight for the entertainment dollar against huge, lavish — and imported — mega-musicals. Magazines, whose numbers and balance sheets had improved dramatically since the legislation of the 1960s that stopped their American competitors from offering bargain advertising rates in publications whose editorial content had already been paid for, faced new pressures from international trade rules, many of them urged by Americans, who viewed such measures as unfair restrictions. Broadcasters continued to make Canadian programs, and in some cases, notably the public networks, even increased their quotas. Our public-affairs programs, newscasts, documentaries, and the hard-edged political satire of such shows as This Hour Has 22 Minutes or the Royal Canadian Air Farce continued to distinguish themselves and tickle our funny bones (22 Minutes often outdrew the newscasts it parodied). But new technologies — the "death star" satellites, the borderless Internet — made it increasingly difficult to find viewers for shows produced on the kind of budgets a purely Canadian audience could support. And on every channel, the American influence crept in, through the "zee" of Sesame Street or the perception of gavels and "district attorneys" as a natural part of criminal courtrooms.*

And so on. When we offered some artificial stimulus — Canada Council grants to give young writers a chance to grow, content rules that forced radio stations to play some Canadian songs (much against their will in the early days), even the magazine legislation — we did fine. But when it was a simple contest of who had the most money to throw around, we were swamped. And more and more, as the world reshaped itself into a global village, and with a political leadership that was either unwilling or unable to mount much of

---

* Two tiny but noteworthy examples of just how invidious these perceptions had become: Early in the years I was writing these columns, my friend Jack Batten published a chatty and informative book about Canadian judges. His Canadian publishers, alas, put a gavel on the cover. (Canadian criminal judges don't use them.) But if Jack had called me through the CBC's automated switchboard in Toronto, a recorded voice would have told him, "If you know the name of the party, press . . . and for zee press nine." Ah, well, the Canadian Broadcast Centre was designed by an American, anyway.

a defence, those who sought to maintain our national distinctiveness felt frustrated and discouraged.

The currents that were engulfing us were not the forces of malevolence. Americans, bless their hearts, wished us no ill. In spite of their own concerns about, for instance, growing Japanese ownership in their beloved Hollywood — or even, heaven forbid, of baseball teams — they never could understand what was bothering us. Don't you want to read *Sports Illustrated*?, they would say. Don't you like Seinfeld? Having trouble with Walt Disney? What's the *matter* with you, anyway?

Well, sure, we liked *Sports Illustrated*; we just wanted a chance to publish our own sports stories (though in fairness we had yet to come up with a successful sports magazine of our own). We liked Seinfeld, too, just as we liked everything from Masterpiece Theatre to Beavis and Butthead — well, maybe from Masterpiece Theater to The Larry Sanders Show. But we also liked The Newsroom, and The Nature of Things and the fifth estate and North of 60 (let alone Hockey Night in Canada, Don Cherry and all), and we wanted a chance to watch them, too. Even Walt Disney and his heirs were fine — as long as they stuck to *The Little Mermaid* and *The Lion King*. But when they took over merchandising the Mounties, wangled their version of Winnie-the-Pooh onto our postage stamps and sent Mickey and Minnie Mouse to be parade marshals of the Calgary Stampede, we were troubled. We *liked* Americans, all right. We just didn't want to *be* Americans.

Not all the forces that were changing our cultural landscape came, at least directly, from outside. As the fever of deficit-cutting swept the land, we looked increasingly to the private sector to run or support functions or activities we had always considered public. Entrepreneurs were selling booze and issuing drivers' licences in Alberta, negotiating to run jails in New Brunswick and funding highways in Ontario. Everywhere, artists turned to corporations and private philanthropists to sponsor their works. Even, in so far minor but nevertheless ominous ways, education was seeking corporate help, from selling advertising space in washrooms or granting exclusive campus distribution to soft-drink companies at universities to providing sponsored computers to undergraduates or, as school boards in Ontario were being encouraged to do, forming "partnerships" with the private sector.

Once again, it was hard to argue that all these changes were for the worse. Most Albertans, for instance — certainly those who lived in affluent neighbourhoods — found shopping for their libations more pleasant at private emporia (though there was some concern about the growing number of armed hold-ups of liquor stores), and no one I knew seemed especially bothered by such matters as Absolut vodka sponsoring a Mordecai Richler story in *Saturday Night*, or the Bank of Montreal subsidizing the Governor General's literary awards. But the ground was shifting. It was now all but impossible to stage a major ballet or an opera without some kind of sponsorship. Across the board, the arts faced a future not unlike that of sports, where beer companies sponsored hockey teams, airlines (and beer companies) put their names on arenas, skiers finished their races by flashing the logos on their skis at the TV cameras and our Olympic athletes modelled uniforms proudly made — and labelled — by Roots.* Even in education, a touch of commercialism, if that's what was needed to keep institutions of learning afloat, was probably better than the alternative. As long as people could sing and dance and go to school, slide down mountains and fall in love with ballerinas, the universe was evolving as it should. But without much debate, we were moving towards a world where the choices of what they sang and where they sang it, which mountains they glided down, which charities were funded and which university courses survived were made not by public consensus or by elected representatives but by corporations, whose only real obligations were, after all, to their shareholders.

The ideas that made Canada were changing in other ways, as well. Traditionally, as regional economies had fluctuated, we had tried to make it possible for people to live where they felt they belonged. If things were bad in Cape Breton, we said, we'll put some public money into letting you stay there till they get better. In the U.S., by contrast, if the cotton mills of the South fell into recession, well, too bad, you could move to the factories and the stockyards of Chicago. Now, as government cutbacks choked off many of the programs that had made that policy possible, we were becoming more like the American model. No fish off Newfoundland? Gee, sorry. We'll tide you over for a while, and even pay for you to pick up some skills that don't have much to do with where you

* Actually, so did HRH Prince William, on a ski trip to Whistler, B.C.

live. But your way of life is over; why don't you just take off for Fort McMurray?

The technological revolution swept over us as it swept across the world. The role of women, though still with an agonizing lack of haste, grew more central to our business and political lives, as did the recognition of gay and lesbian realities. Immigration, now largely from non-European countries, continued to transform the textures and lives of, especially, our largest cities; by the end of the nineties, the *majority* of Torontonians came from abroad. Smoking fell out of fashion. Guns and violence were subject to much debate. Canada's domination of world hockey ended, but Canadians scaled Everest, won the world's bag-piping championship and contrived — and were caught at — the biggest stock-market scam of modern times.

Some of these stories had little to do with the Americanization of the world, but some were part of it. The explosion of technology, for instance, was scarcely anyone's national phenomenon, but in Canada, as with the multi-channel universe of television, or the fact that we now made our airplane reservations (to fly through "open skies") or checked our credit ratings through Atlanta, it was a constant reminder of the American presence. The waves of immigration raised questions again about whether we could — or should — maintain our policy of mosaic vs. melting pot; even some articulate voices in the newer groups — the novelist and short-story writer Neil Bissoondath among them — questioned the wisdom of reinforcing "multiculturalism." In the war against smoking, uncharacteristically — for we were the country that liked to legislate virtue — we lagged behind the Americans, who were proving that in this matter at least perhaps litigation — suing the bastards — was more effective than taxation or banning advertising. Guns and violence were genuine Canadian concerns, though perhaps, in the case of guns, viewed differently in a land of vast spaces where hunting and trapping were a way of life. But even here the American influence was evident. It was possible, for example, to sit in Pangnirtung on Baffin Island, watching the supper-hour news from Detroit, and wonder if a bunch of balaclava-hooded hooligans was about to crash through your hotel-room door; in virtually all of Canada, meanwhile, as the calls for tougher cops and stiffer sentences grew louder all the time,* the statistics for violent crime actually went down.

The attack on the military was part of — and helped to feed — a trend that was at least as evident in the United States as it was here: a decline in the public's respect for all institutions, from politics to the established churches to the media. But in Canada, where a painstaking but ultimately frustrating inquiry into our troops' behaviour in Somalia led to TV photos of such outrages as Canadian soldiers beating their prisoners and senior Canadian officers shrugging off their responsibilities, the assault seemed particularly poignant. The inquiry was cut off before it could get to the core of what had gone

* And when even the Royal Newfoundland Constabulary began to pack their guns by hand.

wrong overseas. But even so, an institution whose proud record had been part of our heritage was besmirched, and yet another blow was dealt against our long-held and distinctive deference to authority.

Hockey? Oh, dear. The Winnipeg Jets and Quebec Nordiques fled to warmer and more lucrative climes; none of the teams that remained in Canada, able to pay their stars only in weakened dollars, appeared likely to win a Stanley Cup in the foreseeable future. Nearly half the personnel of the "National" League, and a significantly higher proportion of the most exciting players, were Europeans or Americans, a statistic that was brought dramatically home at the Winter Olympics in Nagano, where the best team we could assemble lost, alas, to the Czechs. But was all this the Americans' fault? To some extent, maybe — it was hard to compete with the marketing skills of Disney's Mighty Ducks or the television appeal of the Fox network's blue-tailed comet of a puck. But looking back on what happened to our game, as so many people did as these years drew to a close, it was hard not to ask if we hadn't shot *ourselves* in the skates. The game that had caught on in the major markets to the south, after all, was not the elegant, free-wheeling shinny so many of us had played as youths; it was a tough, grinding, shoot-it-into-the-corner-and-see-what-happens exercise that had first been sold as a kind of Roller Derby on ice. Even in the NHL, the Canadians remained the best exemplars of this style. And who was its most notable prophet ("Watch this, kids")? Our own — and the CBC's — Don Cherry.

Ah, well; it felt good to blame him.

If there was one story that was quite specifically Canadian, and which received, perhaps partly for that reason, much less public attention than it deserved, it was, surely, the stirrings of aboriginal power. After more than two centuries of neglect, paternalism, broken promises and unconcealed racism, the first peoples of Canada were at last coming into their own. The diseases brought to their continent by the earliest Europeans had reduced their numbers by more than half but had failed to wipe them out. Now, with one of the highest birth rates in the Western world, and with modern health care and diet making their way to remote communities, they were roaring back; by the millennium, to take just one statistic, more than half the population of Saskatchewan will be of Native descent. A policy of residential schools to turn their children into model Euro-Canadians had failed drastically and cruelly; most — though not all — of the original languages of Turtle Island had survived, however precariously, and some, having skipped a generation when aboriginal languages were beaten out of the residential schools, were blossoming anew among the young. So were many of the old beliefs and customs, often adapted to or reinforced by modern technology; it was telling, for example, to visit some northern communities — sometimes knee-deep in a population that was now more than fifty per cent under sixteen — and see the syllables of Inuktitut or Cree come whirring over the Internet.

For every story of hope or rebirth, though, there was at least one of despair: poverty, substance abuse, unemployment —

sometimes as high as eighty per cent — and intolerable living conditions on the reserves; devastation in the cities. The cores of almost all the major cities in the West were now predominantly — and sadly — Native. But a strong, articulate, educated aboriginal leadership was growing across the country. The courts were recognizing more and more land claims, and in some cases also recognizing the efficacy of traditional codes of justice. In 1996, the most expensive royal commission in our history delivered a massive and eloquent report that recommended sweeping changes. The first reaction of the body politic was to nod in agreement at most of the report's principles, but to dismiss most of its recommendations — especially those requiring an injection of yet more money — as impractical; the aspirations of our first peoples received another blow. For many both inside and outside the Native communities, though, it seemed as if we were turning our back on the inevitable. Changes were coming, and one could only hope they could be brought about without more of the unrest and violence that had cropped up in the years I was writing these columns.

FOR ALL THESE STORIES, and the changes they engendered, I enjoyed one of the best seats in the house. As I'd been for the ten years that preceded them, I was the host of the CBC Radio program Morningside, and for three hours a day, five days a week (though not, mercifully, fifty-two weeks a year), and with the help of an extraordinarily gifted and hardworking network of producers, I was fortunate enough to talk to many of the most interesting players in the public forum, and with some of the best minds in the land about what the players were up to. Morningside was, and its successor This Morning remains, such an eclectic program that trying to summarize its contents is fruitless; as well as politics and economics (foreign as well as domestic), we talked of everything from food to eccentrics — from soup, if you'll forgive me, to nuts. But at its heart it was still what the CBC likes to call "public affairs." The single common theme, if there was one, was that in everything we did we were determined to remain, in the wonderfully felicitous phrase whose origins are described in the piece called "Watson Lake, White Rock, Wolfville," "as Canadian as possible . . . under the circumstances." Sometimes, indeed, the more the country changed in the ways I've tried to outline here, the more important that determination seemed to be.

That was my day job. When I'd finished it, on Friday afternoons, I'd head for Lake Simcoe. On my way, I'd do a few errands and drop in on some neighbours, many of whom appear in these pages. Slowly, the world I'd been immersed in would fade away. In its stead, I'd turn to private matters, and when it was time to settle in to do my column for *Canadian Living*, those matters were what was on my mind.

An antidote to the real world? I'd say the opposite: this *was* the real world — friends, family, adventures, misadventures, places, community. In the words of the media philosopher Neil Postman (an American, alas, but we used to like to talk to him on Morningside), other than the weather, when was the last time you heard anything on the radio that actually changed the way you behaved?

Sometimes, inevitably, the changes in the political climate cropped up in what I wrote: my experience in the health-care system, my reflections on my own laboured attempts at bilingualism, an evening in the presence of Pierre Trudeau. And sometimes the people I met and the places I saw were a function of my privileged position on CBC Radio, or of the travels to the golf tournaments that bear my name. But even in those cases, I would think of a conversation I had had — on the radio, to be sure — with the Montreal management guru Henry Mintzberg. What Canada needs, Professor Mintzberg had said, as we talked of constitutional matters, is "an open-window policy." We should cancel our newspapers for a while and turn off the television — maybe, heaven forfend, even the radio — and *look out the window*. If we did that, he said (I'm paraphrasing a bit), we'd remember what the constant chatterers of the media and the political élites all too often forget: that whatever its flaws this is a great country, the envy of the world; that people, living in an infinitely beautiful and still under-appreciated landscape, get on with each other; that, under whatever circumstances, being as Canadian as possible is a goal we are blessed to aspire to.

WHEN I HAD FINISHED my writing — usually on Sunday evenings when I was at Lake Simcoe, but other times when I was roaming around — I would fax them to Julia Armstrong at *Canadian Living*, and I am grateful to her for the care, professionalism and unfailing good cheer she exhibited in nursing them through to publication. As much as I hate to admit it, Julia's changes to make my words fit into their confined space often made them read better, as well, and even here, with a chance to undo her handiwork, I have almost always bowed to her judgement. I am grateful, too, to Bonnie Cowan, the editor who hired me at *Canadian Living* in 1986, and whose support and friendship I have cherished ever since. And, as always, I am grateful to Edna Barker, who has become irreplaceable in my life as an author. On a final note, I'm pleased that *Canadian Living*'s fact checkers come in for a mention in these pages. I'm sorry only that I can't blame them — or Edna — for whatever bloopers I've managed to add here. There aren't many things I can do for myself, as you'll discover as you peruse these columns, but messing things up is one of them.

P. G.
Lake Simcoe (of course)
Summer, 1998

PART ONE

Friends

Mr. Dressup, He's Our Man

THE AIRPORT TERMINAL at Cambridge Bay, N.W.T., a wooden structure about the size of a small-town McDonald's, was crowded. A group of us were on our way south — a couple of hours south to *Yellowknife*, if you want an indication of how far north we were — after a few days of singing, reading, dog-sled racing and golf-on-the-ice, and about half the town, or so it seemed, had come to see us off. On the incoming flight were some Members of Parliament who'd come to look at the DEW-line site, whose eerie, bulbous buildings loom at the edge of Cambridge Bay, and to figure out what to do with it now that the Cold War is over. One of them, it turned out, was the member for my own riding in Ontario. She introduced herself and said she had a literacy project for the summer she wanted to talk about. She asked about our visit to Cambridge Bay. I told her some of the details.

"You mean you've got *Mr. Dressup* with you?" she said, and all thoughts of politics were over.

It was like that wherever we went. The flight attendants on Air Canada and NWT Air (Arctic char and caribou for snacks), the people who shepherded us around as we gathered at our southern rendezvous, the clerks in the hotels, *everyone* in Cambridge Bay, and even the rest of the well-known people who came with us —"can I have my *picture* taken with him?" bubbled the poet Sheree Fitch before they'd even shaken hands — wanted to meet Mr. Dressup. I've never seen anything like it. Cambridge Bay was our sixth expedition into the North to play golf for literacy, and over the years, I've invited a whole cornucopia of people to come with us. They're role models, and we, and the northern literacy people, exploit them shamelessly. I've taken hockey players (Ken Dryden once, and Randy Gregg), Olympians (Silken Laumann) and musicians (Tom Cochrane and Murray McLauchlan), poets, actors (Cynthia Dale and Sarah Polley) and children's writers (Jean Little came with us this year, with her guide dog, Ritz, and the effervescent Sheree Fitch is almost a fixture on our tours) and maybe the best role model there is for kids north of sixty, North of 60's Tom Jackson. They've all made an impression; the kids, and often the adults, have enjoyed, and, I'd like to think, been affected by them all. But Mr. Dressup, who is in real life a sixty-seven-year-old suburban Torontonian named Ernie Coombs, is in a league by himself. People — Canadians —*love* him.

Know the strangest thing about him? This most Canadian of our folk heroes is actually an American, or was, till he took out his citizenship in 1994. He was born and raised in Maine, and started in the children's entertainment world with Mr. Rogers. When Mr. Rogers came to Canada in the early sixties, Ernie came with him. When Mr. Rogers went home, Ernie stayed, at first on Butternut Square, and then, for twenty-eight years, as Mr. Dressup.

The CBC, I think, did two incredibly smart things. One was to keep him in Canada. The other was not to tinker with him, or with Casey or Finnegan or any of the rest of his friends. He was just . . . well, Mr. Dressup: soft-spoken, friendly, respectful of his audience. He fibbed once, he recalls now, but he won't say when or about what. Otherwise, he was a constant among the chaos. The more gimmicky and commercial — not to say violent — the rest of children's TV grew, the deeper he dug into the Tickle Trunk.

In person, he's exactly as you'd want him to be, as shy and self-effacing and polite as he is on the screen. He's funny, too. When the CBC in Inuvik called for some results of our golf game, they asked someone else how he'd done. "Lost a few balls," said the golfer.

"And what did *you* lose, Mr. Dressup?" said the interviewer as Ernie Coombs came on the line from our hotel.

"My reputation," he said for all the Arctic to hear.

I don't think so. As Sheree wrote just before we left, and as all the rest of us chanted, too:

Mr. Dressup, he's our man,
Makes us feel we really can,
Makes us feel Ca-na-di-an.

Geoff: Joined at the Hip

HE IS ABOUT MY AGE, and the leather jacket he is wearing is not unlike my own.

He catches my eye. I smile distractedly. There is something very familiar about him. But, preoccupied by the people who have lined up to have their books signed, I can't place him.

I am already under a spell of *déjà vu*. I feel like the Old Dutch Cleanser label, the one that shows a woman holding a can of Old Dutch Cleanser, and on the label in the picture is a woman holding a can of . . . and so on, spinning ever inward on itself.

I was here four years ago, almost to the day, in the Wellington Street Book Shoppe in the town where I grew up: Galt (Ontario) then; Cambridge now.

Then as now, I was signing books. People kept stepping out of my past, from the town I had left more than forty years earlier. When I got home that evening, I wrote about the memories that came tumbling back. After that column ran, I heard from all over the country, not only from people who'd grown up in Galt, but from others who'd left other home towns, and found echoes of their own lives in what I'd written. When I put together a collection of columns,* I included that piece. And now, four years later, here I am again, signing the book that includes it, sitting at the same table, and here, again, come the memories, sometimes from the people who were here in 1989 ("Did you have to put me in the sentence right after you talked about the, er, French safes they made at General Tower?" says Tom Brown, who used to live two doors from me) and sometimes from people simply bearing news: Frank Ferguson, I learn from his granddaughter, the English teacher who had such an impact on so many of us so many years ago, lies in hospital, aged eighty-seven, and . . .

Suddenly, I have it. I break from the spell at the signing table and turn to the man in the leather jacket. "You're Geoffrey Johnston," I say.

"And who," he says, as we break into simultaneous grins, "did you think I was?"

---

* *Canadian Living: Selected Columns*, McClelland & Stewart, 1993. This is a classic case of completing the circle, I guess: column, book, column, and now a book again. I wonder if I'll be able to get back to Galt to sign this one.

Geoffrey Johnston — *William* Geoffrey Johnston, as probably I alone in this room know. He is not just "about my age"; he is precisely ten months older. His birthday is September 4. His address was 5 Lansdown Avenue. His phone number was 416-R (which became a minor complication the year we were in grade eight, and had overlapping crushes on the beauteous Ann Vale, whose number, since her family shared a party line with Geoff's, was 416-J.) His mother, widowed, was Madge — Aunt Madge to me, as mine was Aunt Margaret to him.

From about grade three, when we were in Miss Durward's room at Dickson School, until our early teens, when I left Galt, Geoff Johnston and I were best friends as only kids can be. We shared *everything*; we were, as Geoff says now, "joined at the hip."

Five days a week, we walked to school together (5 Lansdown was right on my route) and played together after four. On Saturdays, we pooled our allowances to go to the matinee at the Palace or the Capitol or the Grand, and talked afterward of Abbott and Costello and Johnny Mack Brown and all the dirty Nazis of the war. In spring, we explored the countryside, getting soakers in the burbling creeks. ("Do you remember," he says now, "the time we found a trapline out near Barries Cut and sprung all the traps with sticks?") In summer, we rode our bikes to Willow Lake, and splashed together off the shallow shore. Winters we skated, weekend mornings on the hockey rink — or, one magical day when a snap freeze coated the world with ice, out across the landscape; Friday evenings, when we were old enough, with girls.

We discovered girls together, as we discovered smoking (I don't know which of us got dizzier), Frank Sinatra and shooting pool. I was at his house the day Roosevelt died, and, on VE-Day, we decorated our bikes together (his was blue, with balloon tires) and rode down Queen's Park Crescent whooping for joy — and the day off.

Sometimes, like all best friends, we fought. Even at sixty, Geoff tells me, he can still trace with the tip of his tongue the scar inside his lower lip that marks the time I raised my head when we were wrestling and bopped him under the chin, driving a tooth into the soft flesh. But we made up. We became brothers. The year we read Ernest Thompson Seton's *Two Little Savages*, we ceremoniously pricked our thumbs and mixed our blood.

It's time to leave. Geoff and I scribble our addresses for each other and walk together to the door. Instinctively, I put my arm around him. He hugs me back. We have, I realize as we prepare to say goodbye, scarcely talked of the years that have passed since we met — scarcely mentioned wives, grandchildren, careers.

"You're taller than I remember," he says now.

"It was a long time ago," I say. "A lot has happened since."

"But some things never leave you," he says.

"No," I reply. "Not even when you think they've gone."

Sandy: Who He Was

ALEX SPEAKS FIRST, Sandy's oldest son, with a younger brother — half-brother, actually, for Sandy was married more than once — at his side.

Alex would be, what, thirty-two now? He's the same age as my Maria. When we lived next door to each other, long ago, they used to play together, and one time, when they were about four, the two of them found an open can of silver paint in the alley behind our houses, and generously and gloriously decorated a neighbour's car. It's a legend in both families.

Now, he's speaking at his father's funeral. As he begins, he's funny, as Sandy was, and as, I'm sure, he'd want him to be now. He talks of a trip he and his dad took together, back to Vancouver, Sandy's old home town. They shared a hotel room. Just as Alex was drifting off to sleep, Sandy began to work on his laptop computer. Alex does a little imitation of the sound: *click-click-click-click-click-click*. Alex raised his head. "Sorry," Sandy said. The room fell silent. Alex nodded off again. Then, just as sleep began to roll over him once more, *click-click* . . . silence . . . *click-click-click-click* . . . silence . . . *click-click-click*— furtive little bursts that, at the time, drove Alex to sleepless distraction, but now, recreated, send ripples of appreciative chuckles through the chapel, for even as the son describes the scene, all of us who knew the father can see him once again, pecking away at his keyboard, his head cocked at some inner joke, not wanting to disturb his son, but still unable to resist the urge to write.

Sandy — his by-line was Alexander C. Ross, but no one ever called him anything but Sandy — was quirky and compulsive and irreverent. He was fifty-eight when he died. He'd had a couple of bad strokes, but seemed to be recovering. Then, when he went home from the hospital — this was typical, too — he took his wife, Minette, to the movies. When the lights went out, as his friend Alan Edmonds says at the funeral, so did Sandy. He went, as Alan says, the way he lived, with panache.

Sandy did *everything* his own way. We met as student editors, he at the *Ubyssey* in Vancouver, I in Toronto. His paper could be as whacky as he was. When the Vancouver *Sun* launched an advice columnist named Penny Wise, Sandy invented Pound Foolish for the *Ubyssey*, and when the world was going crazy over marathon swimmers — this was the year Marilyn Bell conquered Lake Ontario — Pound Foolish, in a blaze of flashbulbs, swam clear across the lily pond on the UBC campus. But, like Sandy, the *Ubyssey* could be serious, too. He won, as I remember, the national award for editorial writing that year.

There was always music around him, often of his own making. He played drums and piano and four-string banjo and, even as a student editor, dashed off little ditties on the topics of the day. Forty years later, I can still quote from "God and Social Credit," his classic on the W. A. C. Bennett government.

Later on, at *Maclean's*— I'm proud to say I lured him there not long after we both got out of school — and in a lot of other places, he changed business writing in Canada, made it sprightlier and more personal. In the seventies, he and a couple of partners bought a moribund monthly magazine and turned it into the lively — and profitable —*Canadian Business*. At other times, he ran *Toronto Life*, tried his hand at a daily column, co-wrote the report of a Senate committee, knocked off a few books and dabbled in radio and television. Whatever he did, he did well, and usually as no one had ever done it before.

Yet what strikes me at the funeral — and it strikes me hard — is how small a role Sandy's professional accomplishments play in the eulogies. Speaker after speaker, following Alex, dwells not on the awards and the achievements but on the man. They talk more of stories he lived than stories he wrote, of how he was always ready for new adventures, of how he loved women — and loved Minette the more for that — of musicians he discovered, of things he said. In a moment that could only have occurred at *his* funeral, someone remembers a discussion of where people wanted their ashes buried. When it was Sandy's turn, he smiled apologetically at Minette and said, "Would sprinkled over Carly Simon's bathwater be out of the question?"

Now, as the service nears its end, I look around. The place is *jammed*. It's overflowing. It is, I realize, a gathering of the tribe: the people who have written or edited or broadcast much of what Canada has read or watched or listened to over the past several decades. You could fill a library with what we've turned out.

Still, I'm thinking about other things. It's time to leave now. As we begin to file out, each of us, at Minette's request, takes a red rose from in front of the altar, dozens of flowers for Sandy's memory. How many of us, I wonder, have felt, or spread, the kind of love and laughter Sandy leaves behind him now? When our turns come, will the mourners talk of what we did or who we were?

I head for home. That evening, I hit the telephone. I want to talk to some friends. We leave, I think, too many important things too long.

John: A Couple of Grey-haired Grandfathers

CONSIDERING THAT JOHN GIRVIN and I were thrown together by happenstance, and that we came from as different backgrounds as we did, the wonder is that we got along at all, let alone laid the cornerstone of a friendship that would last, so far, nearly half a century. This was, needless to say, many years ago, when John and I, teenagers, found ourselves at Ridley College, in St. Catharines, Ontario, a boarding school for (then) boys. We were both in grade eleven, and both out of sync with the rest of our class. John had come from Detroit; because Ridley had underestimated either his Michigan education or his intelligence, they had started him off in grade ten and promoted him only in the late fall, making him, of course, the new kid in the class all over again. I hadn't shown up at all until after Christmas, when my home life in Galt had crumbled — my latest report card had me twenty-seventh in a class of twenty-seven — and with a background that included draped trousers and ducktail haircuts, felt out of place among the flannels and blazers of boarding school. We were assigned to the same dormitory and took refuge in our mutual solitude. The next year, we stuck together, and stayed roommates until we graduated.

We were a pretty odd couple. John was (and is) tall and muscular, a gifted athlete who rapidly converted the baseball skills of his American boyhood into a starring role on the Ridley cricket team. I limped along behind him. All through the summer before our final year, I diligently practised throwing a football, hoping I could succeed to the vacant and envied position of Ridley quarterback. John, meantime, had missed football the year before, after a swimming accident (he was also a swimmer of near-Olympian ability). When we returned in the fall, I asked him to play some catch. The coach saw him throwing the ball back to me. My quarterback aspirations ended on the spot, and John began a football career that would take him to the leadership of the storied University of Western Ontario Mustangs. I started smoking behind the gym.

Academically, we went our separate ways, as well. I outscored him at languages and math, as I remember (the discipline of boarding school did wonders for my marks), while he excelled at such arcane (to me) subjects as zoology and chemistry. He worked harder than I did, and in our graduating year was rewarded by being appointed a prefect — a kind of noncommissioned teacher with disciplinary powers. He was a very decent and honest young man, who could easily turn aside my tendencies to sarcasm and irreverence.

Whatever our differences, the friendship grew. At night, we would lie awake in our room and talk of girls and dreams and teachers and home; we came to know each other well and, I think, to like what we found.

After Ridley, our lives took widely different paths. He went to Western, I to the University of Toronto. We seldom saw each other. Once, during a football weekend, I took him to my fraternity house and, to the anger of my "brothers," showed him the secret scar of my initiation. Then I dropped out of university for a while and he soldiered on, through medical school, on to a PhD and postdoctoral research. For a while, each of us, now married, lived in Montreal and we visited from time to time, but he was tied up in neurological research and I in writing for *Maclean's*. We went to one Ridley reunion together and discovered that not only had our friendship survived but so had our sense of being outsiders.

And now, so many years later, we find ourselves on the same university platform — at Western, where John continues his research and his good works (he is a brilliant neurosurgeon). We both speak, and each of us refers to our shared background and tells stories of the pranks we used to play. We grin at each other across the podium, a couple of grey-haired grandfathers in flowing robes with a lot of memories to share.

Afterward, we retire to the Girvin household, and through a long, warm, laughter-filled afternoon, the talk seems to carry on from where we left off in 1952. When it's time for Gill and me to go, John's gracious and lovely wife, Betty, says, "You two should hug."

"Nah," we say. "Guy thing."

But we do anyway — awkwardly and self-consciously but with long-lived and lasting affection.

A Call from Rhonda

THE PHONE MESSAGE, taken by a receptionist, was a bit confusing—"Roda? Ronna?" with two different numbers, one a 1-800 and the other apparently (514) in Montreal—but I had no doubt as to who had called, and I smiled with pleasure as I thought about her and how good it would be to hear from her again. I dialled 1-800 and asked the operator to connect me to the number in 514.

I remembered the first time I'd called her, in 1977. I was writing for the *Toronto Star*. At one point, looking for some relief from a gloomy and political winter—and, to be honest, to get a few easy columns—I started a little contest. Write me, I asked my readers, about how you'd spend tomorrow if you knew it would be the last day of your life. Among the responses, which were full of romance and imagined adventures, one letter stood out. A young woman, a university student, I guessed, had put together a day of various delights, all of them touchingly simple.

Now, nearly twenty years later, her letter and its sprightly, joyous tone still lingered in my mind. She wanted one last ride on the Ferris wheel at the Exhibition grounds, I recall, and to go to the Mars restaurant on College Street for a bran muffin and to dance (was it to jitterbug?) in the living room with her brother. Her name was Rhonda.

Before I called her, I did some digging around. Yes, Conklin Shows would be happy to open the Ferris wheel for a winter ride, and yes, the Mars would be happy to see her, and yes . . .

The lady who answered the phone turned out to be her grandmother. "Rhonda's out at school right now," she said. (I'd been right about university.) "You'd better tell me what you want her to know."

"Couldn't I tell her myself later on?" I asked.

"Sure." Her grandmother laughed. "But you'd better do it in person. I guess you didn't know Rhonda doesn't hear."

Now the operator from the 1-800 number — it's called TDD, which, to Rhonda's dismay, stands for Telephone Device for the Deaf (she prefers "hearing impaired") — came back on the line. "Sorry," she said. "I let it ring, but there's no answer. That doesn't mean anything, of course. Unless people have lights in every room they don't always know there's a call."

I remembered a restaurant dinner years ago when Rhonda wanted me to meet the man she planned to marry. "I wish you'd trim your moustache," she'd said. "Sometimes I can't *hear* you."

After our day on the Ferris wheel and eating bran muffins, Rhonda and I became friends. I *really* liked her, right from the start — bright, chipper, totally undaunted by what she never seemed to think of as her handicap. She'd had minimal hearing since childhood. She made her way through life and school by lip-reading, and danced to the rhythms of the music she loved. Her speech is clear, though the consonants are sort of rounded, as if she has a slight and exotic accent. She finished university and set to work as a teacher. She did marry the man she introduced me to — a handsome and brilliant scientist (I spoke proudly at her wedding, taking care to face her as I proposed the toast, and danced the *horah* with her friends and family) — and has gone on to a life in two languages. She has two daughters now — one born, to my delight, on my birthday — and with our separate lives, we had, until this spring, kind of lost track of each other. I've been working at Morningside, which of course she's never heard, though she's followed me, it turns out, through this column.

I tried the 1-800 number again. Whatever it's called, TDD has been a blessing for people who have hearing impairments. The hearing caller speaks with an operator — they're all bilin gual, too — who types the conversation onto a screen in the client's home.

"Your party is there," said the operator.

"Rhonda?" I said, and spelled my name.

The operator read her message to me.

"Yippee," she said. Taking some liberty, I added an exclamation point on my own.

A Group to Hit Golf Balls With (4 letters)*

ALTHOUGH I NEVER MANAGED to meet Eva Eliza May Walden of Owen Sound, Ontario — Aunt May to her nephews, nieces, grandnephews and great-great-nieces, Mother Walden to her neighbours — I knew, when I read of her passing, she'd been a member of my club. My club is huge, you see, so big that no one knows its total enrollment. And since we never hold meetings or collect dues we never know when we'll run into a fellow member, even if, as with Mother Walden, who was eighty-three when she died, it's only after a member is gone and it takes a newspaper obituary to tell us proudly that "she was able to finish the cryptic cross-word in the *Globe* up to last Friday."

---

* "Club," in case you're not used to cryptics.

My own trek to membership in the cryptic crossword club started years ago when I was living about an hour out of Toronto and commuting as a passenger. The editorials, the comic strips, the sports, the horoscope — even the news in the *Globe and Mail* I picked up on the way could never last the whole trip, and in desperation I began to work on the mysteries of the puzzle. Like all outsiders, even those who've mastered regular crosswords — who know that a "tor" is a hill and "cos" is a kind of lettuce — I was, at first, totally baffled. Cryptics are a maze of anagrams, puns and hidden clues, and although there are supposed to be two different ways to arrive at each answer — in one I have just finished, for instance, the word "Morse" is defined as a "means of communication [the code] for a TV detective [Inspector Morse of the BBC]" — until you twig to some of the tricks you might as well be playing in Albanian. You don't have to be a genius to solve a cryptic, you just have to know the lingo. My own breakthrough didn't come until I'd gone back to work on the radio, and my studio director, a brilliant reformed lawyer who shared my pleasure in both games and words, initiated me into membership. I was hooked.

Now, I'm a full-fledged member. Six days a week, I begin my mornings — kick-start my mind, I like to say — with the cryptic in the *Globe*, still the best in Canada, though in the minds of the membership not as pleasing as it used to be when Saturday's was composed by the scholarly Alan Richardson. When I'm out of the *Globe*'s circulation area and I can't find a local puzzle, I arrange for another member to fax it to me.

And when it's Sunday, I either settle for the *Toronto Star*, which has a not bad cryptic, to tell you the truth, or reach into one of the books my thoughtful children give me as presents. Once, when I bleated on the radio about the *Globe*'s puzzle having been repeated in error one morning, leaving me without my daily fix, my fellow members Frank and Olwin Nelson of Thornhill, Ontario, whom I have never met, faxed me a copy of quite a clever puzzle they'd drawn up for their friends.

Senior members of the club use more than just the fax. In the chapter that has come together in the smoking room of the building where I now work (one of the only things I'll miss when I finally beat the weed), there are a couple of techno-whizzes who have learned how to pull the puzzle from the deliciously difficult British *Daily Telegraph* off the World Wide Web, and there are copies distributed around our favourite table.

There are some things members never do. Perhaps the most grievous sin is to tell a fellow member an answer without being asked for it. I learned this to my chagrin one day a few winters ago, when I blurted out on the radio the answer to, I think, 5 Down that morning, and the switchboard lit up with calls from angry members who hadn't yet got to their daily chores. When two or more members are working on their separate copies, though (at the lovely old house in Nova Scotia, where a gang of us hunker down each summer, we actually buy three copies of the *Globe* so each of the members among our number can have a clean puzzle), it is sometimes permissible to trade one of your answers for another from someone else.

We are, by and large, a happy band. I know of at least two Governor General's Award winners who start their days with cryptics — the novelist Timothy Findley and the poet Dennis Lee — but I know of all kinds of other people, too, from race-track handicappers to TV technicians. And all of us, I'm pretty sure, would like to have it noted when we leave the club forever that we, too, had solved the cryptic till the Friday before our departure.

Oops! Check That, Would You?

FOR A GUY who's earned his living with words for more than forty years, I certainly get a lot of them mixed up. Is it "seperate" and "desparate," for example, or "separate" and "desperate"? Sydney, British Columbia, and Sidney, Nova Scotia, or the other way around? I can *never* remember if the naturalist and writer whose stories and drawings meant so much to me as a kid was Ernest Seton Thompson or Ernest Thompson Seton, or if William Wilfred Campbell's classic poem "Indian Summer" (which he wrote when he was an undergraduate at the University of Toronto, by the way) begins "Along the line of smoky hills/The crimson forest stands" or if the hills are crimson and the forest is smoky. These aren't hard. It's just that I can't get them right.

Fortunately, I'm a great looker-upper of things. I have a spell checker on my computer, a shelf full of reference books (including the new *ITP Nelson Canadian Dictionary of the English Language*, which tells you which words are Canadian and which aren't; Mr. Zamboni, alas, who invented the machine that clears hockey rinks, came from California, the editor tells me) and my newest and most cherished toy, *The Canadian Encyclopedia Plus* on CD-ROM, with which you can do anything from watch Donovan Bailey win his Olympic gold to translate a few sentences into, or from, French.

So, okay, I know (for the moment) that it's separate, desperate, Sidney, B.C., and Sydney on Cape Breton Island; that it's Ernest Thompson Seton; that Campbell's hills were smoky and his forest crimson.

Sometimes, though, you're just too rushed to look things up. Once on the radio, just after Bill Clinton had made his first inaugural address, I said the speech was okay but that Clinton was no John F. Kennedy. "Who could ever forget," I pontificated, "'Ask not what you can do for your country; ask what your country can do for you'?" Well, *I* could, obviously, since this memorable phrase — or memorable, apparently, to everyone but me — goes precisely the other way around, of course: "Ask not what your country can do for you . . ."

And sometimes you're just too stubborn. The most amazing thing about my latest lulu is that I whizzed the *Canadian Living* copy department. This is not easy to do. *Canadian Living* takes its facts very seriously, which is one of the things that makes it so reliable to read and such a pleasure —

even when it's occasionally annoying — to write for. The fact checkers, unsung heroes of the editing process, check *everything* and, over the years, bless them, they've saved me from moving towns I've lived in, from messing up the ages of my children and, once, from killing off a guy in Winnipeg whom nature hadn't got around to.

But I got them this time. I wrote about the widespread but secretive club of people who do cryptic crossword puzzles. I told of a couple named Frank and Olwin Nelson of Thornhill, Ontario, who had heard me whine on the radio about the *Globe and Mail* having repeated the previous day's puzzle that morning, keeping me from the daily habit with which I kick-start my mind. Frank and Olwin, I said, had been good enough to fax me a copy of a homemade cryptic they do for their friends — another example of the fellowship of our membership, even when we haven't met.

"We can't find them," said the *Canadian Living* fact checker. "We want to make sure of the spelling of Olwin's name. We've called all the Nelsons in Thornhill."

"Oh, for heaven's sake," I said. "Trust me for once. I don't have their original fax, but I do have the notes I made from the letter they sent me."

As soon as that column was published I heard from my friends again. "Dear Peter," they faxed me. "At first we thought you had made a mistake but then we realized what you are up to, you trickster. You are sending cryptic messages to us. . . . This one is particularly clever because it is baked into an article about cryptics. We think Olwin Nelson is an anagram [cryptic puzzles use a lot of anagrams] of the words *sell*, *win*, *noon* and that your next message is going to give us a hot tip on the stock market. . . ."

There was more — all of it as clever and as charming as had been the original puzzle they sent to me.

The fax was signed Frank and Olwen (sic) *Dixon*.

Oh, dear. At least I got the Frank right. Sorry, Dixons. You're terrific people. And sorry, fact checkers. You're terrific, too, even if you never trust me again.

Celebrating Our Own

FETCHINGLY DECKED OUT in walking shoes, chinos, a turtleneck under her sweatshirt, Jane Jacobs makes her way to centre stage. It takes her a moment to settle into her armchair — she is, after all, eighty-one — but even as she does so, the audience that has packed the Music Hall theatre on Toronto's Danforth Avenue fills the air with its love and respect for her. People have come from all over the world to honour her — from China, from Africa, from Scandinavia and Latin America, from all parts of her native United States and her adopted home of Canada. The conference, which extends for nearly a full week, is called Jane Jacobs: Ideas That Matter, and at every learned discussion and through every scholarly paper, the ideas that have resounded the most deeply come from Jane's own writing (everybody calls her Jane) about cities and communities. Although she disdains the personal attention and is uncomfortable with celebrity, she revels in the exchange of thoughts, and this afternoon, as she sits in her armchair awaiting a kind of debriefing on the day's sessions, her eyes are twinkling over what one newspaper has described, accurately, as her "apple doll" cheeks.

I sit beside her, a bit intimidated by the sweep of her knowledge and the brilliance of her mind, but basking in the warmth of her presence, and flattered and pleased to have been invited to ask the day's questions. I've just returned from Calgary, I say, and have missed most of the discussions. But even in Calgary, I tell her, people are talking about the conference and the fact that planners and architects and environmentalists and virtually all who care about the life of cities are talking about her recognition as the pre-eminent philosopher of urban life of our times. "I think," I say, "that I've seen more of you on television this winter than I have of hockey." "Perhaps," she replies, without missing a beat, "but my season is much shorter."

Our conversation begins with a meeting she held this morning with a group of schoolchildren on what they wanted in a Toronto of the future. She is delighted that they listed both a candy factory and a place to process potato chips — she thinks it's important that cities produce for themselves the things they used to import — but is at least as pleased that they emphasized clean air and water. But as we talk, we touch on everything from "biomimicry"— the way humanity can learn by imitating nature — to the fact that she still likes to wish upon the stars. When we finish, the audience rises to salute her, and as she prepares to sign some books for them, her eyes are still twinkling.

The trip to Calgary (from which I've just returned) has, by coincidence, had a similar feeling. What took me there was a chance to be part of an evening of celebration of the novelist W. O. Mitchell. Though Bill, as I've called him for nearly forty years, was gravely ill and unable, alas, to attend his own evening of honour, I'm sure the warmth and the love and the laughter reached out from the Max Bell Theatre — again jam-packed — to where he lay, and that he knew the writers and poets and theatre people who gathered to read from his works or tell stories of his influence or his unquenchable humour all felt a debt to him and wished him well. He has long been a hero of mine, as well as a pioneer of Canadian writing, and the evening of tribute was a particularly moving occasion.*

And then, on the Saturday after my conversation with Jane Jacobs, I am in Peterborough, Ontario, where the tribe of Canadian writers, as Margaret Laurence used to call them, has assembled in a stately dining hall at Trent University to pay tribute to Timothy Findley. It, too, is a lovely evening. June Callwood, another writer — and, indeed, another hero of mine — speaks. Margaret Atwood reads a sprightly verse she has written for Tiff and his companion of more than thirty

---

* In the spring of 1998, a few months after this column appeared, Bill Mitchell died. I miss him deeply and mourn his loss. But I'm glad he did hear of the evening we gathered to send him our love.

years, William Whitehead. Veronica Tennant dances, Sylvia Tyson sings, Joe Sealey plays piano—all for a writer we admire and cherish. When it's over, Tiff rises to speak his thanks. We, in turn, rise for him.

Three occasions to lift the spirit, for people who have mattered to us all. I wonder, driving back to Lake Simcoe, if we have learned at last to celebrate our own.

Cooking with Bonnie, a First Course . . .

BONNIE STERN, COOKBOOK AUTHOR, cooking-school owner and, in my view, one of the nicest people there are, opens my refrigerator and takes out the fresh Atlantic salmon we bought earlier in the afternoon. She whisks together a marinade of black bean sauce (from the same shopping expedition), honey (ditto), and about half a cup of the apple and carrot juice she has found, miraculously, in the fridge. She spoons the mixture over the fish. "Here," she says, "massage this in." "Massage?" I say. "Sure," she says, and demonstrates with her supple fingers.

As I give the salmon its zesty rubdown, Bonnie checks the oven. We have already spread a baking sheet with parchment paper (both the sheet and the paper are new acquisitions) and covered it with two pounds of plum tomatoes, cut into wedges; a pair of red peppers, split, cored and de-stemmed and laid out flat, skin-side up; one onion, peeled and quartered; four shallots, peeled and halved; and, most enticingly for me, a whole head of garlic, with its top sliced off and placed, bottom up, at the centre of our papered pan. We've sprinkled everything with olive oil, kosher salt and freshly ground black pepper (Bonnie, aware of my predilection for pepper, had arranged for me to get what she called the perfect mill — a little machine with easy entrance for the corns on top, a handle at the side for grinding and, at the business end, a removable transparent collection basket), preheated the oven to 450°F, slid the pan in, reduced the heat to 425° and turned to other culinary pursuits. Now, as she opens the oven door, the kitchen smells like a Mediterranean summer.

We are, Bonnie and I, in the early stages of what I'm calling my "cooking makeover." Even though I confess, sometimes, to preferring the before pictures to the afters when magazines remake someone's hair, make-up and wardrobe, I've decided this is what my cooking needs. Much as I enjoy it, it's become too boring, More to the point — and more honestly — here in the Toronto apartment I share with Gillian Howard, Gill has been preparing virtually all the meals, while I've been saving my own kitchen adventures for our country retreat. I approached Bonnie, a friend, with my makeover idea. She agreed enthusiastically — Bonnie, so far as I know, does *everything* enthusiastically.

We started with an inventory and a general heave-ho. Out went all the tired old spices — even the half jar of filé powder

I'd searched all over Toronto for after I read a recipe for gumbo in a Lillian Hellman book years ago. Out went everything stale or in the freezer for over a year. Out went all those mysterious concoctions at the back of the fridge, utensils I never use and gizmos whose purpose I've long forgotten. It's amazing, I couldn't help thinking, what builds up.

And then we went grocery shopping. We met at a midtown supermarket and, for the next hour, prowled the aisles. We had a really good time. One of Bonnie's most recent and notable cookbooks, done in conjunction with the Heart and Stroke Foundation, is called *Simply HeartSmart Cooking*, and that's how she shops: reading labels for the fat content, choosing one-per-cent milk instead of two, picking, nearly always, fresh over packaged. When we were finished (I, used to shopping more like a European housewife than the head of a Canadian household, spent more money in one session than I usually spend in a week — but saved a lot, too, with her sage advice), we headed for the apartment to try some of the armload of pots and pans she'd brought from her cooking school.

Now, dinner is almost ready. As Bonnie puts some water on to boil in the pot she had brought along with its colander-like lining, which has, she says, "the holes in the right spots," I trickle some oil — not much — into my new, ridged grill pan. As it heats, we take the vegetables from the oven and pick out enough for the pasta; the rest will be the basis of dinner tomorrow. I chop some fresh herbs onto a plate with balsamic vinegar, salt and pepper, then toss it with the pasta and selected vegetables and, ceremoniously, squeeze the roasted head of garlic over the lot. Just before we put the salmon on, I call Gill at work.

"You should come home," I say. "Something's happening in our kitchen."

A Second Course . . .

FRESH HERBS ARE GENERALLY BETTER than dried, if you can find them, and you should chop them fine; and if you save the stalks from the rosemary you can use them as spears for barbecuing shrimp. Eat breakfast, even if it's just some fruit and a bagel you've kept in the freezer and thawed in the microwave. To open a mango, cut off two opposite sides as close to the pit as possible, then cut a grid pattern into the flesh of each piece down to (but not through) the skin; gently push the skin to turn the fruit inside out. To flavour couscous, add some rice vinegar and a dollop of frozen orange-juice concentrate. Rinse basmati rice until "you can count the grains through the water," then measure a cup and a half of water for every cup of rice, bring it to a boil, cook on medium high till you can't see any water, then cover and cook on very low for another ten minutes; sprinkle some rice vinegar on it when it's done. To juice a lemon, first roll it under your palm against a firm surface, pressing down to break up the pulp.

Read labels when you shop, even for things like crackers; a good general rule for such items is that there should be only three grams (or less) of fat for every one hundred calories. Buy *two* kinds of balsamic vinegar, one at a moderate price for such things as marinades, and another better-quality one for salads or fresh strawberries; if you do a taste test you'll see why. Splurge on authentic Parmigiana-Reggiano cheese, too (a little goes a long way); pinch your pennies elsewhere. Buy kosher salt; it's coarser and sprinkles well from the fingers. When cooking, wash your utensils as you go. Eat bran.

I know these things — and more — from the cooking makeover I embarked on a while ago with Bonnie Stern. My plan was to have Bonnie — who runs a cooking school and writes cookbooks, and is as nice a person as I know — go through my kitchen, throw things out, replenish the larder with tastier stuff (I can't imagine buying black bean paste or hoisin sauce on my own) and, generally, set me on a new course.

It's working, though in ways I never would have expected. After our first shopping excursion and the dinner of grilled Atlantic salmon, pasta and roasted vegetables, Bonnie and I went hunting and gathering again, this time to a fishmonger she likes — you should trust the person you buy your fish from, she maintains — and a greengrocer's in midtown Toronto. We shopped carefully and with pleasure, discussing how we'd prepare each ingredient. Then, back in my refurbished kitchen, we rolled up our sleeves and went into something of a cooking frenzy.

Just for fun, she said, Bonnie had brought with her a tiny chicken, perhaps two pounds, and with it — she laughed as she brought them out of the box — a pair of ordinary house bricks. As I put the rest of our purchases away and cleared the countertops for the rest of our chores, she split the bird up its breast, removed the backbone, laid it out flat, dusted it with salt, pepper, rosemary and thyme, rolled it in a little olive oil, heated the ridged grill pan she had me buy — perhaps my favourite among my new utensils, by the way, since it emulates the results of an outdoor barbecue — wrapped the bricks in foil, set them on top to flatten the chicken and prepared to grill it over medium heat for about twenty minutes a side.

Even while the chicken simmered (we were to put it in the fridge for later consumption), Bonnie and I began preparation for other future meals. We marinated a linen-white centre cut of sea bass in garlic, rosemary, brown sugar, balsamic vinegar (the cheaper brand), oil, salt and pepper. We trimmed and cut up some juicy shrimp and scallops for a pasta. We whipped up some couscous orange juice and all and rinsed some berries for dessert, carefully placing the raspberries on top of the sturdier blueberries. And, last — and best — of all, we roasted vegetables.

I love doing this, it turns out, and enjoy finding new combinations of garlic, fennel, tomatoes, peppers, potatoes, onions, slices of squash, baby carrots, cauliflower florets, eggplant, zucchini — and even, if you put them in for the last twenty minutes or so, such surprises as green beans and asparagus. We (for Gill has taken up the pastime, too) do this now at least once a week, laying a foundation for a variety of pastas and salads — healthy, delicious, easy to do. Bonnie's advice has not only made over our kitchen and our diets, it has rejuvenated them. We learn more — and eat better — all the time.

And a Third – with Elizabeth

OTTAWA. A WINTER SATURDAY. I wake in the most luxurious hotel suite I've ever seen: bedroom, two bathrooms (one big enough to open a health club in), living room, sitting room and two (count 'em, two) bathrobes inscribed with the crest of the Westin hotel.

The Westin, thank heavens, is one of the sponsors of the event I've come to town for. They're looking after the chefs. But who, I ask myself, as I pad about amid the splendour, pays for these things when they're not freebies? Lobbyists? Cabinet ministers? Kings?

Better question: what am I doing here? Some months ago, Elizabeth Baird, to whom I have a hard time saying no, asked if I'd speak at a literacy dinner that was to be held in conjunction with the prestigious International Wine & Food

Festival in Ottawa. While I was there, Elizabeth said, she and I could make an appearance together at the show. We could cook something. Why not? I said. Since then, however, the dinner has been cancelled, and only the cooking date remains. Which is why I'm staying in a chef's accommodations and why I'm now due at a demonstration kitchen to stand in front of a lot of people, all of whom, I'm sure, since they go to food shows, can cook better than I can.

Oh dear. At least Elizabeth will be there to see me through.

Eleven a.m. Elizabeth, it turns out, and a whole lot of other people: a cordon — cordon bleu, I guess — of professional, or at least experienced, cooks and food writers.

And what have they done to me, I wonder now.

The menu is to consist of my own beef stew, first unveiled in this column years ago,* along with an orange and watercress salad and some cheese scones. I'll do the stew, presumably, while Elizabeth and the cordon handle the salad and the scones. That's okay; I cook my stew all the time. Yet, earlier this Ottawa morning, while I've been relaxing in solitary luxury, my associates have laid everything out in preparation for my adventure. All the ingredients for my stew — carefully checked and quantified by the experts of the *Canadian Living* test kitchen — are spread on the cooking surface before me, each in its own perfect container: the beef (already cubed), the flour (sifted and measured), onions (cut trimly into eighths),

---

* And subsequently published in *Canadian Living: Selected Columns*. For a reprise, see pages 75–76.

leeks, garlic, carrots, parsnips, butter, olive oil — everything, right down to little plastic cups of salt, oregano, basil and, one of my essentials, sherry. Furthermore, on a stove backstage, a pot of "my" stew, pre-prepared by the pros, burbles aromatically for lunch.

Smiling her winsome smile, Elizabeth hands me an apron, clips a microphone to my sweater and turns the podium over to me.

Trouble is, this is not the way I cook at all. If anything, in fact, it's the precise opposite.

Measure? Me? If I'm baking, perhaps. But for a *stew*? Oh, no, members of the cordon. Check my column. We don't measure. And we certainly don't lay everything out. No, my dears, we *create*!

But there is no backing down now. I plunge on in the only way I know how.

First of all, I say, I can't flour this lovely beef in a metal bowl. *I* start at the liquor store, where I buy my sherry and from which I keep the paper bag.

Presto, someone brings me a brown paper bag.

I scoop a brimming handful of flour into the bag, grind some pepper on top, toss in the cubed beef and shake everything vigorously together. Elizabeth compliments me on my two-handed technique.

Encouraged, I bungle on.

"Away with that cube of measured butter," I cry.

A cordonette brings a pound. I chunk some directly into the pan.

"And bring me the *bottle* of olive oil. And, while you're at it, the sherry, too."

I slurp and cut, hack and sauté, using a wooden spoon to stir the browning beef, garlic, onions and leeks in the bubbling oil and butter.

"Don't *worry* it," Elizabeth says. But now in full flight, I am oblivious to her sage advice and stir some more. The members of the cordon work around me, whisking away the empty containers, finding the right knives, responding to my every carefree whim.

"More garlic!" I cry. Then, turning to the audience, I proclaim, "No dish in history has ever suffered from too much garlic."

To my astonishment, I hear a smatter of applause. Do they actually think I know what I'm *doing* up here?

And so it goes. The more manic I get, the calmer Elizabeth and the cordon seem to become. While I've flailed away, they've mixed the scones and put them in the oven to bake. The salad has, miraculously, been tossed; my messes, by equal magic, tidied. It looks for all the world as if we do this all the time.

Noon. Time for lunch. The cordon goes backstage to get the precooked stew.

"It's all right," says Elizabeth. "We'll serve this one first."

Twelve-fifteen. Reviews from the crowd are positive, even enthusiastic. For myself, I'm too excited to eat. Maybe I'll have some later, back in my suite.

IN CASE YOUR TWO PAGES of my first collection of columns are as splattered in sherry and beef stock as mine are:

¼ cup unsalted butter
¼ cup extra-virgin olive oil
1 cup flour
Fresh ground black pepper
1¼ lb lean stewing beef, cut into 1½ inch cubes
1 bunch green onions
2 leeks
5 cloves garlic (or more)
Sherry (about 1 cup)
1 tin beef stock
Pinch oregano
Pinch basil
2 parsnips
3 carrots
1 tin (19 oz) whole tomatoes
1 tin whole, peeled potatoes

In a large skillet over medium heat, melt the butter and olive oil. While butter melts, place flour and freshly ground black pepper into a paper bag. Add beef chunks and shake vigorously. Pick out each piece of beef by hand and place it in the pan. As it browns, peel and chop the onions into eighths. Chop the white part of the leeks into one-inch pieces. Chop the garlic. Add garlic, leeks and onions to beef. Reduce the heat and let cook, stirring occasionally with a wooden spoon. When the meat is brown, splash in about a cup — who measures? — of sherry. Add beef stock. Add oregano and basil. Lower the heat another notch (you don't want to *boil* the stew) and let it simmer for about twenty minutes. Peel the parsnips; scrape the carrots lightly. Cut parsnips and carrots into Brazil-nut sized pieces and add them to the stew. Add tomatoes, liquid and all, let simmer for another thirty minutes, then add potatoes. Heat for fifteen minutes and serve with a fresh baguette.

Lisa: Hairdresser Guilt

HER TOUCH, I DISCOVER, is gentle. She combs me lightly and, without bothering to more than suggest the elusive line where God has tried vainly to give me a natural part, trims the sides and back with her small scissors. Snip, snip. Pleasant. I'd pore over my notes if I were wearing my glasses. As it is, I just lean back and enjoy the attention. Only when she is happy with the length does she reach for the electric clippers and begin the tidying up. Buzz, buzz. Still gentle, but I'm nagged by guilt.

She — her name is Gail, but the world calls her Freddie — has done hair much more famous than mine. She is a mainstay of the flourishing industry that swirls around film and television production in Toronto, freelancers who move from job to job or, as they say in the business, shoot to shoot: camera operators, technicians, bright-eyed, multi-skilled youngsters working their way in. There are similar enclaves in Halifax and Vancouver, among other places, and everywhere the HMU people (that's hair and make-up, to the uninitiated) are part of it. Freddie, typically, does whatever's required — wigs here, period beehives there, a platoon of long-haired actors to transform into Gulf War marines — never losing her good humour or teasing, sometimes flirtatious, sense of humour. Everyone who comes into our studio seems to know — and to like — her. I like her, too. It's just that . . .

This is television's fault. Twenty years after my first unhappy foray into hosting a program of my own — a late-night talk show — I have decided to give it another try. This time, I'm determined, things will be different. No band, no studio audience, no glaring lights — and as little HMU as I can get away with. Just me talking with interesting people, on a set I feel comfortable with; we've hung it with Canadian paintings, some of which (the cheaper ones) actually belong to me. It's *conversation*, or supposed to be, for which I still think there's room on TV. And, so far at least, I'm having a good time.

For all my convictions about trying to be myself on the screen, as opposed to the blow-dried, painted mannequin I turned into the first time around (my hair looked as if you could pick it up like a helmet and take it to its own dressing room), I've made some concessions. Even I know you can't be *too* natural in front of the camera. Let one collar point stick out and that's all anyone looks at. So I have snazzy new shoes, some slacks that seem to fit and even socks (with both halves of every pair the same colour!) long enough to hide my unglamorous shins. And make-up — just a dab of powder, please — and, with Freddie, hair as my producers would like it shaped.

She reaches for the moisturizer and begins to massage it soothingly into my beard. And all I can think of is Lisa.

Lisa lives and works in my village on Lake Simcoe. Her shop is called the Mane Idea and, corny name or not, I've been going there regularly for about five years. Switching *to* her, for goodness' sake, was hard enough. For years before that, I went to the fabulous Carmen in downtown Toronto, where I was tended with old-fashioned luxury, aromatic lotions, shoulder rubs and all. But Lisa, who charges $16.05 for both beard and hair and can squeeze me in between permanents, was just more convenient; I could walk to my appointments. But I still felt badly about Carmen and never did screw up the courage to tell him I'd moved on.

And now here I am, being unfaithful to *her*.

"There you go, love," says Freddie, having given me a once-over with her blow-dryer and sprinkled a light spray of fixative over my errant locks, which she has left, at my producers' instructions, longish at the back.

I slip into one of my fancy new sweaters, being careful not to muss my coiffure, and head for the set. I look all right, I think, stealing a glance in a mirror. I hope Lisa — and Carmen — will approve.

Anyway, I resolve, I'm going back to the Mane Idea this summer. It's not only that I like Lisa so much, and appreciate the village news we exchange on every visit. Or even that she's the very model of an independent entrepreneur, slugging it out all day in a business she's building for herself. It's the guilt. She's my hairdresser, after all.

Molly: A Dangerous Woman to Know

IF JUNE CALLWOOD SHOULD EVER slow down — and even those of us who regard her as indefatigable in her numerous good works know that some time that day must come — I think I know her successor. She is Molly Johnson, a mixture of siren and pixie — in a cocktail gown she is as sultry as Lena Horne, but in jeans and a sweatshirt, a much more common costume, and with her relentless, infectious grin, she looks more like your daughter's best friend. Molly lives in, and sings out of, Toronto, but her gifts and enthusiasm are known, at least in the music community, as widely as her causes.

Molly is a dangerous person to know. I met her about a decade ago when she was in her early twenties. She is the daughter of an ex-American football player and a Canadian political activist. Their house in Toronto was an endless scene of politics and show-biz gossip. Everyone from Eldridge Cleaver to Billie Holiday stayed there on the way through town. The kids started performing as tots and, in one way or another, have kept at it. But Molly is the busiest. Over the years I've known her, she has fronted a rock band, sung jazz with Oscar Peterson, starred in a memorable series of Blue Mondays, for which she sang old ballads (you can hear those Billie Holiday visits when she sings the blues), and had her own week at the glitzy Imperial Room of the Royal York Hotel.

But what makes her dangerous to know isn't her talent, which every musician I know thinks is much greater than she realizes — she just has to find the right métier — it's her energy, her generosity of spirit and her ability to enlist others to her various causes. Even when she was in her twenties, she seemed more interested in drawing attention to other young Toronto artists — playwrights, poets, painters — than in talking about herself. She was a moving force in much of the Canadian musical scene's opposition to South African apartheid. She's done everything I've ever asked for literacy — I can still see her last year in Rankin Inlet, her first time north of sixty, on the phone to see if she could get some local sculpture shipped south to an art gallery she knew of, lining up some teenagers for a video on AIDS in the North, and infecting everyone she met with her good spirits. And when she asks, which she does all the time, there is simply, as I know from happy experience, no way to turn her down.

When you meet her she can seem scatterbrained. Her ideas are so fertile, her imagination so untrammelled, that you can think she's out of her depth. She never is. Her crowning achievement, of course, is the annual series of concerts called Kumbaya, which raises money for AIDS hospices. Kumbaya is totally Molly's brainchild. A few years ago, she just grew tired of seeing all the energy that went into international AIDS benefits and said the equivalent of "Hey, kids, we could put the show on right here." Right here turned out to be Ontario Place in Toronto, and the "kids" ranged from Molson Breweries to MuchMusic to a who's who of Canadian popular culture — from the Barenaked Ladies to Doug Gilmour, then of the Toronto Maple Leafs, whose return call from the Leafs' dressing room so pleased Molly that she kept it on her answering machine. Under Molly's inspiration, Kumbaya has also spread to T-shirts, calendars and a marvellous recording of participating musicians, which, typically, omits any of Molly's own music. The result, so far: some $500,000 for AIDS relief, though Molly was working on it so hard that she ran out of rent money and had to move, once again, halfway through last year's preparations.

"So what?" said Molly. "It was great, eh?" It was, too.

When Kumbaya was over last fall, it was time for other matters. Three days later, in fact, there was a party in Toronto for PEN, the international writers' organization. One of the key figures there was — of course — June Callwood, who had also — of course — lent some of her energies to Kumbaya.

After the drinks, PEN needed someone to sing. "Will you introduce her?" June asked me. "I think you know her."

"Yes, I do," I said. "Ladies and gentlemen, Molly Johnson, working for another good cause."*

---

* It may interest you to know that Molly makes another appearance here. She is one of the brides in the piece called "Swallow Point 1: On Passages and Places," page 203.

Tom: The Spirit Spreader

WE ARE RUNNING, NOT SURPRISINGLY, a little late. We started as scheduled at eight o'clock — well, almost as scheduled; it took a while to seat the capacity crowd — but since then a lot of the performers have run over their allotted time. Why not? it's hard not to think. These people love what they do, and many of them are tired from the gruelling travel. If Tom had enforced the rule he learned years ago at the Winnipeg Folk Festival, there'd have been no encores. But as it is, there's just too much good feeling to ask anyone to stop. People are singing, and the audience is cheering them on.

Charlie Major, for example. Not everyone in the audience is a country music fan, but Charlie's warmth and showmanship have won them over. Or Melanie Doane. Melanie, a singer, songwriter, fiddler and all-round musical protégée — her father is J. Chalmers Doane, who built the Halifax ukulele chorus — has been, like Charlie, with the whole tour, but here in Toronto, to her own delight and everyone else's, her husband, Ted Dykstra, one of the two creators and star of the brilliantly funny *2 Pianos, 4 Hands*, has come out to play keyboards for her, and she has sung a song he wrote for her. It's a lovely evening.

As far as I know (which is pretty far, actually, since a lot of friends of mine are involved) they've *all* been lovely evenings. This is Tom Jackson's Huron Carole, a travelling series of concerts that has now spread across the country like the spirit of Christmas itself. It took them a while to get going. Tom, who is, as I wrote long ago, as good a man as I know, first held one in Toronto in 1987, trying to raise both money for, and awareness of, the homeless and the hungry.* It sort of fizzled. But Tom, undaunted, tried again the next year, in his hometown of Winnipeg, where, in an earlier incarceration, he'd been down and out himself. The concert worked, but the homeless were wary, and Tom and his friends and his incredible wife, Alison — who has become as important to the whole movement as Tom himself — cruised the streets to find takers for the meal they'd set up for Christmas Eve. But since then, wow! There are now Huron Caroles (I don't know where the *e* comes from) from Victoria to St. John's. From the admissions,

---

* Also in *Canadian Living: Selected Columns.*

the sale of souvenirs and CDs, and donations received from such national sponsors as Syncrude and Nova, they'll raise about $250,000. But because the food banks to which the money goes know how to leverage cash, that means more than $4 million in food for the hungry. And they still eat on Christmas Eve.

In a better world, of course, we wouldn't need this kind of effort. In this one, alas, we do. Even as stock markets went through the roof and the banks — the ones that deal in money — made profits in the billions, nearly one out of every ten Canadians used a food bank at least once this year, and, to our national shame, forty per cent were children.

Here in the Music Hall in Toronto, though, it doesn't feel like fulfilling a social obligation. It feels like a party. And a Christmas party, at that, as all the performers add a carol or two to their usual repertoire. Tom and Alison remain the core, but sometimes it seems as if every musician in Canada wants to take part. Some — the Maritime country singer Joan Kennedy, for example — hitch on for whatever part of the tour they can manage. Others drop in when the Carole hits their town, and over the years everyone from the Rankin sisters to Shannon Caye (who also works in the Carole's Calgary office) to Prairie Oyster has come to sing and play.

Tonight Cynthia Dale has dropped in to join Tom in a beautiful rendition of "O Holy Night," the others singing along backstage. Now Tom, resplendent in a dinner jacket, leads everyone in the title hymn, his rich bass voice bringing deep resonance to the old words, first written — in Huron — more than three centuries ago. "'Twas in the moon of wintertime," he sings. We join him — even I. It's Christmas, and some, at least, of the hungry will be fed.

Coach Peter: A Guide on the Way Back

WHEN COACH PETER COMES TO CALL for me at my apartment, he is already in his working clothes, which in his case consist of sweatpants, a nifty pair of striped gym shoes, a light sweatshirt and, depending on the weather, a colourful, usually crested, windbreaker. I'm geared up for him, too, though not as athletically natty. (Not as athletic, either, but that's another story.) I wear my own sweatpants — though I wish I could find a pocket to put my key in — one of a whole wardrobe of celebratory sweatshirts I seem to have picked up over the years (World Ice Fishing Championship, Lake Simcoe, Canada; N.W.T. Literary Council, with slogans in nine northern languages; Guess Who's Coming to Dinner, from the lovely birthday party *Canadian Living* threw for me a few years ago, signed by all of my gorgeous guests — from Debbie Brill to Alice Munro) and, since Christmas, when my daughter Alison hunted down a pair for me and Coach Peter (unaware that my family had joined my cheering section) brought along another set as a present, my own striped walking shoes. In either pair, I feel as if I ought to be able to slam-dunk a basketball.

The highlight of my getup, though, is not visible to the eye. Around my chest, against my skin and just beneath the lettering on my sweatshirt, is a soft strap, about the width of a belt. On my wrist is what appears to be a wristwatch, and, indeed, it does display the digital time. But if I have dampened the inner side of my chest strap properly, to make contact between my skin and the strap's electrodes, and if I push a small button on the side of the watch, the digital display turns — miraculously — into a display of my heartbeat.

Coach Peter, as you will have guessed by now, is a personal trainer. I heard about him a year or so ago, through a doctor I'd been seeing to try to get some meat back on my bones and some spring back into my step. It took me several months before I worked up the nerve to call him. "Personal trainers," it seemed to me, belonged to the world of ladies who lunch or corporate executives with overweight expense accounts. But as I asked around, I found that real people use them, too — even if it's by joining a fitness club, or, as some friends of mine do, forming a little group to split the costs. Most of all, though, I just thought nothing could be a better investment for me than getting some of my health back.

I have not, for much of my life, been a good tenant of the body God and my parents started me out with. Too many cigarettes, too much wine, too little sleep, too little exercise. It's been fun, but I've paid for it. If I had it to do over again, I'd . . .

Ah, well, I don't. Coach Peter smiles in greeting at my apartment door — he is virtually always cheerful — and we head off for the exercise room. There we — or I, although I've come to look on our sessions as a team effort — start slowly, usually on the treadmill. I walk; Peter coaches, controlling the speed of the belt and its possible uphill grade, always keeping an eye on my heart rate. (He wants it under 130 beats per minute; if I go over that he slows me down.) At first, I was discouraged by some of the other residents of my building, many of them middle-aged women, who strode or jogged on the adjoining treadmill for several hypothetical miles while I huffed and puffed at the pace of a lumbering platypus. But after a while, I realized it wasn't a contest, and both my times and my measured distances began to improve. After my stationary walk, I do some stretching (never, as Peter says, to the point of pain), some "crunches" (sort of semi-sit-ups), some easy lifting (with both arms and legs) before I head to the showers. The whole process takes about an hour, and we try to do it two or three times a week. Some workouts are better than others, but Peter seems to sense when to push me ahead and when to ease off. However I do, he never lets me get disappointed.

I wish I could report a miracle has transpired, and that I'll be ready for the 2000 Olympics. No such luck. But I've put some muscle mass back on, I sleep better and walk more sprucely. It's a long road back. I suppose I could have started by myself. But I didn't, did I? I'm glad — and lucky — I have such a congenial guide.

Alex and the Chickens

GIVEN THAT I HAVE BEEN dealing with Alex the butcher for close to a decade now, and that in that time I have come to know — and like — not only the vittles he sells me but the way he runs his business, it should probably not have surprised me that, when I asked him one day about the source of the chickens whose richness of taste so many guests in our house have commented on over the years, his answer contained not only the name of his supplier but a brief history of the family behind it.

"It's King Capon," he said. "They've been raising chickens for generations. As a kid, I worked for the father of the guy who runs it, Tom Appleton, and Tom and his wife, even though their kids are in charge now, are still out there in the barn every . . ."

Alex — his last name is Gallacher — is the same. Gallacher's Quality Meats is a *family* business, and virtually every product on its counters bears its mark. Alex, and sometimes young Alex, as everyone calls his son, butcher all the meat themselves. His wife, Ann, makes meat pies and sausage rolls and frozen stews — they make their own chicken stock, as well — and, when she's home from university, young Angela, who has a smile that would light Saskatchewan, makes coleslaw or assembles kababs, marinated in garlic and paprika and some other things the Gallachers won't tell me. There are mounds of creamy potato salad and stacks of juicy spareribs, trays of spicy farmer's sausages, a counter of sandwich meats (including their own stuffed pork roast) and, on some of the shelves, homemade sauces and preserves that young Alex, who takes after his father, has begun to package under his own label.*

But it's the chickens, at least at our house, that draw the most enthusiastic reviews — plump and juicy and redolent with flavour. "They're ugly," as Alex says — they're tinged with yellow as opposed to the bland white of supermarket birds —"and they're not cheap. But they taste like *chicken*."

"Free range?" I asked.

"Not really," Alex said. "Tom raises his in a barn. But they hop around all the time, and they eat mostly corn."

I eat *them* in a number of ways. In summer, I like to barbecue

---

* Since I wrote this piece, Alex Senior has stepped down (as I have from Morningside) and young Alex has taken command. The old guy still comes in on Saturdays, though, and the chickens are still delicious.

their succulent breasts and meaty thighs — the fact that I am, as I pointed out many columns ago, the best barbecue cook in the history of the world may well have something to do with the place where I buy my raw materials — or else bone the breasts and experiment with something light and fancy.

But it's now, when the weather's nippy, that I enjoy my chickens most. This is roasting season and, inspired by the quality of what I work with, I have, I think, developed a roasting system that ranks with my barbecuing skills. Here's the heart of it.

First, I make a stuffing of roughly equal parts (I *never* measure) of sliced leeks, diced celery or celery heart, and cored but not peeled Granny Smith apples, liberally sprinkled with sage (*plenty* of sage), rosemary, sometimes thyme, occasionally oregano. If the mood strikes me, I'll add half an onion or so, or perhaps some pecans. Never bread crumbs.

Then (and this is my favourite trick) I peel and julienne (to pencil thickness) four parsnips, four fresh carrots and three or four (depending on the size) potatoes. I take the chicken from the fridge, cram the cavity with the stuffing and lay the chicken on its back in a ceramic roasting pan. Then I tumble the vegetable pieces — they should be about an inch and a half long — all around the chicken, reaching to the side of the pan. Now — and most important — I scatter the vegetables with spoonful-size gobs of butter. My theory of butter is the same as Joe Ghiz's theory of the lemon in his famous Caesar salad: "When you think you have enough, add that much more again."

And that's it. Into the oven at 425°F; turn the heat down immediately to 325° and roast for exactly twenty minutes a pound. Perfect. I may, in fact, open a restaurant.

Or would, I guess, if I came from the right family.

Gloria and I, at Sixty

"GOOD MORNING," I say to Gloria Steinem. "I see you're not naked yet."

The most beautiful — and probably most famous — face in the feminist movement does not blanch or smile. "And that you haven't," I stumble on, "dyed your hair purple or . . ."

No smile yet. But a flicker of recognition. A moment's silence as she gathers her thoughts.

We're in the Morningside studio in Toronto. Steinem is in town to talk about her latest book, a collection of essays called *Moving Beyond Words* (Simon & Schuster, 1994).

I am, ordinarily, leery of this kind of interview: best-selling American authors, slogging through the book tour, turned by its rigorous schedule into conversational automatons, determined only to mention the title of their book a few times and move on to the next stop. But Gloria Steinem, I know from experience, is different. For one thing, she actually engages you in conversation — listens to your questions and, even when they're dumb, tries to answer them. For another, and unlike a lot of other Americans, she understands she's in a different country.

"You're referring," she says now, with the hint — at last — of a grin, "to the poem I wrote about —"

"Yes," I say, perhaps too eagerly. "Where you ask the 'Goddess' to give you the 'courage to walk naked at any age, to wear red and purple, and . . .'"

I have, to tell you the truth, been looking forward to this occasion for some time. In many ways, Steinem's life and mine have been parallel, starting in magazines, moving to other fields. We are also, I happen to know, exactly the same age. And this year — it's the subject of the most penetrating essay in her book — Gloria Steinem (and I) turn sixty.

She has been — dare I say this?— important to me over the years. I began to read her in the 1960s. Even now I remember her account of working undercover (so to speak) as a *Playboy* bunny. From the outset, I liked her style, the way she often couched her increasingly militant feminism — she didn't really join the movement until she was in her thirties — in terms that made you laugh as well as think. I remember, for instance, an essay she wrote about what the world would be like if men menstruated, how it would be a badge of honour rather than, as it then was, a source of embarrassment. (There's a similar piece in her latest book, which suggests that if Sigmund Freud had been a woman, we'd have had to cope with the idea of womb envy.) She was, among other things, the perfect answer to anyone who thought being feminist meant being drab and earnest and anti-male, and she shaped and influenced a lot of people's thinking, including, though I didn't always agree with her, mine.

I came to know her a bit — not well, but in the way people in my business get to know their subjects. The first time I met her, I discovered how vulnerable she could be, when, on an old black-and-white afternoon TV series, I noticed her hand was shaking in nervousness and, still uncomfortable myself, reached out across the camera to hold it for a while.

She's different now, of course, a kind of pied piper of her cause. She spends more of her life on public platforms than some of us do in bed. But she still has to conquer her shyness every time she rises. "If I can do this," she likes to say, "anybody can." Once again, I know exactly what she means.

And now, she says, she feels good about being sixty, the way she felt good about entering her teens or her twenties — a new stage. She looks forward, she has written, to the "upcoming pleasures of being a no-holds-barred, take-no-guff [actually, she doesn't say guff] older woman."

Maybe she's right, I think, as she's been right so many times. If a woman, albeit an extraordinarily attractive one, can look so positively on entering the back nine of her life, what reason has any man to sing the blues?

Buoyed by her confidence, dazzled by her charm, I decide once again to remind her what kindred spirits we are.

"And weren't we smart," I ask, "to have been born in 1934? Boy, when you and I started in the magazine business, there was no one between us and the top. Why, before I turned thirty, I was the —"

I stop cold. The most beautiful face in the feminist movement is looking askance at me. Before I even finish the sentence, I realize how stupid I must sound.

I'm right, to be sure — about myself. But I'm a man. When I signed on at *Maclean's*, at the age of twenty-four, I was an instant editor, with two people — women — reporting to me. There was a better writer than I'll ever be still working on the reception desk and another who, making less money when she left than I had started with, had just gone to *Chatelaine*. Four years later, my way unblocked, I was managing editor.

Things are different now, I realize, and, though not perfect, better. But if Gloria Steinem, who helped to change them, had shown up where I was working when we were young, she might have been my secretary.

Now I Remember: Louise

SHE IS LOVELY. Tall and slim and dark, wearing a white cocktail dress that shows off her burnished skin. I know I have seen her before. But I can't, for the life of me, remember who she is.

We are outside the Regency Ballroom of the Hotel Saskatchewan in Regina. A gala evening lies ahead. The Saskatchewan Writers Guild has teamed up with provincial publishers and librarians to hold the first-ever Saskatchewan Book Awards. They've invited me to give what the program calls "a presentation," right after the saskatoon berry pie. I'm honoured but, as the moment grows closer, not sure what I should say.

Who is she anyway? She's looking at me now, giving me the kind of quizzical appraisal I sometimes receive from women of her age (she's in her thirties, I would guess) just before they approach me, ask me if I am who they think I am and, when I confirm their speculation, say, without hesitation, "My mother is your greatest fan." But this is different. Obviously, she knows me. Who . . .?

I am no good with names. My excuse is I meet too many people. But the truth is I just have no knack for it. I am to remembering people what the tone-deaf are to music.

Once, also at a literary dinner where I was due to speak, and also in Saskatchewan, I sat next to the lieutenant-governor. We'd met, actually, just before the dinner began, when he and his wife and the premier — Grant Devine, in those days — and *his* wife and I formed a receiving line. His Honour and I chatted all the way through the fruit-stuffed quail, the cold strawberry soup ("The chicken was small but the dessert was terrific," said someone I know) and the buffalo steak. Then, just as Premier Devine was finishing his introduction to my speech, the lieutenant-governor brought out a copy of one of my books and asked me if I'd autograph it for him. And — well, you can guess the rest. "To His Honour, a Great Canadian," I scribbled desperately. (He was, in case you're wondering, the Hon. Frederick William Johnson, a former chief justice of the province who, for all my faulty memory, truly *was* a great Canadian.) Another time, on a book tour through Vancouver, I was so moved by the sensitive and probing questions in one particular interview that I wrote a long and heartfelt dedication to the reporter — and finished it with a name that wasn't hers. Still another, I spoke for ten lyrical minutes, singing the praises of a politician who was running for mayor of Toronto, and then, when I got to the climax — and even after I'd gone well into overtime hoping it would dawn on me — couldn't come up with her name.

"It's Louise," says the woman in the white dress now, and, suddenly, I not only remember who she is but know what I should talk about this evening.

Louise Halfe is a poet and, if I'm any judge, a good one. She was, in fact — and this is where I met her — the poet laureate of one of my golf tournaments.

The poets laureate of golf is probably the best idea I ever had. I had it in 1986, when I invited Dennis Lee, the Governor General's Award winner and best-selling children's poet, to spend the day with us at the first tournament we ever held and, when we were finished, to make a poem about the occasion. Dennis's work was such a hit that I've kept on with the idea ever since. I've had Margaret Atwood and Susan Musgrave, Sheree Fitch and Lorna Crozier, Antonine Maillet and (bless her memory) Bronwen Wallace. I've had novelists (David Adams Richards) and folksingers (Valdy wrote a piece called "Read Between the Lines," which has become a kind of anthem for literacy) and, once, a woman who'd never written a poem before but who'd learned to read and write through money we'd raised by playing golf. And three years ago in Saskatoon, I had Louise Halfe, who lives there with her doctor husband.

Everywhere we've been, the poems — and the poets — have been a smashing success. And, when the pie has been served, that's what I talk about now: how poets give voice to our thoughts; how we should listen to what they have to say; how, as I've learned through the golf tournaments, nothing has really happened until someone has written a poem about it.

The speech, if I may say so — it is, after all, a literary occasion — goes over rather well. When I finish, the organizers make me a little presentation: one of the original illustrations from a book I've admired called *A Prairie Alphabet*. I admired it so much, in fact, that when it was honoured at the Mr. Christie awards for children's literature earlier in the year, where I also spoke, I wondered aloud how I could have one of the pictures.

"You remember that, don't you?" says the illustrator now, laughing.

"Of course," I say.

"And," she says, "I'm sure you also remember that even when you were asking for it you couldn't remember my name."

"Why, it's Yvette," I say quickly, glancing at the signature. "Yvette Moore." Then, seeing who else has approached the podium, add, "I wonder if you've met Louise."

Mick: A Lesson in Growing Up

NO, I ASSURED MICK AND JULIA over breakfast, the fact that I had lost my credit card was not Her Majesty's fault. We were in Victoria, at last summer's Commonwealth Games. The evening before, as the, ahem, master of ceremonies of an event called A Mid-Summer Night's Gala, I'd had the honour — pleasure, really — of presenting a number of Canadian performers to the Queen and a lot of other dignitaries (it had taken me about five minutes to get through the list of honorifics that began with Your Majesty, Your Royal Highnesses, Your Excellencies, Prime Minister and didn't end until I got to Ladies and Gentlemen, Mesdames et Messieurs). The evening had gone rather well, if I may say so, although the brilliant tenor Richard Margison, who actually comes from Victoria but now travels to opera companies all over the world (he'd had to beat his way back from Australia for the opening of the Games), had burst into "God Save the Queen" just a moment or two before the subject of his anthem had reached her seat, so the royal party had had to linger in the aisles as he sang (if you can linger at attention), and when Cape Breton's marvellous Ashley MacIsaac, wearing his kilt, had broken into one of his characteristic step dances as he fiddled, his socks fell down. Still, I'm sure, there were some royal — or at least vice-regal — toes tapping and smiles all around.

And now my credit card was missing. I had no idea when I'd lost it. I keep it, usually — I know this not very smart — in the hip pocket of my everyday pants. Before the concert, I had changed into my best bib and tucker in the trailer I shared with Richard Margison (like all classical singers, he's a good guide to the rigours of the stiff shirt) and after it, still in formal attire, we'd been whisked backstage for a little royal walk-past. (Prince Edward wanted to know if that was *really* "Amazing Grace" that Susan Aglukark had sung in Inuktitut.) Then, when I returned to the trailer, there was my card, as they say in Newfoundland, gone. Stolen? Hard to imagine. The security people at the gala had practically outnumbered the audience, and anyone skulking around, presumably, would have faced life in the Tower of London. No, as I was saying at breakfast, it was not Her Majesty's fault. More likely, I'd just dropped the card somewhere as I was fumbling nervously with my cummerbund.

Wherever it was, I was in a pickle. Like a lot of people, I use my card not only to pay bills but to keep myself in cash;

I've actually come to *like* bank machines. But this morning, the day after I had met the Queen, I was half a continent away from home without enough change in my pocket to buy a paperback for the plane, let alone get my car out of the airport parking garage when — or if — I returned to Toronto.

And that was when Mick rode to the rescue.

Mick — you may remember him from my account of his and Julia's wedding a year or so ago — is my youngest. He's nearly thirty now and, based in Vancouver, is well on his way in a career not dissimilar to my own. It was a broadcast assignment, in fact, that had brought him to the Games. But I still can't help thinking of him as the baby of the family, the funny one, the one the other kids — who love him dearly — all like to tease.

And now, as we scraped the last of our scrambled eggs from our breakfast plates, the baby of the family was offering to lend me money.

"No, Mick, I couldn't," I said. "You *need* what you have in your pocket."

"I'll get by," he said. "Think of all the times you bailed *me* out of—"

"But I'm your *father*," I said. "That's what fathers do."

"Please," he said. "I'd really like to." He slipped me sixty bucks. I swallowed what I thought was my pride, and stuck the folding money in my pocket. Mick grinned. So, I confess, did I. Even fathers, I guess — even those who get to dress up in fancy clothes and host gala evenings for the Queen — can sometimes use a lesson or two on growing up.

P.E.T.: The Last of His Kind

EVEN IN PROFILE, which is the only view I can manage from the edge of the standing-room-only crowd in the lobby of Metro Hall in Toronto, he is magnetic. His skin is the colour of fine parchment now, but the bearing is still regal: the noble set of the head, the high cheekbones, the aquiline nose. Staring at him — as is, I realize, almost everyone else in the room — it is hard not to picture the expression that must be on his face: aloof, with a smile, perhaps of superiority, flickering just beneath the pale surface. I remember at the old *Star Weekly*, in the middle of his incredible rise to power, we found a photograph of a bust of Machiavelli and ran it next to his portrait. Trudeau and The Prince. They looked like brothers.

He is seventy-eight now, which means he was in his early forties when I met him, though everyone thought of him as younger. I was in Montreal, writing for *Maclean's*. He was an elusive but influential figure in the city's intellectual life, still removed from partisan politics but very much a part of the Quiet Revolution. I approached him to see if I could write a profile of him. He was less than enthusiastic (even then he seemed indifferent to the press) but eventually he invited me to meet him at his mother's house, high on the shoulder of Mount Royal. I showed up about ten in the morning. He answered the door himself. "A drink?" he asked. "Well . . ." I said. He poured me four fingers of straight Scotch, and I sipped away as we chatted, my head spinning — and not only from the excitement of his ideas. Years later, I reminded him of the occasion: "I thought you Quebec intellectuals lived pretty bohemian lives," I said. "I thought all you Toronto journalists were alcoholics," he replied.

I can remember virtually every occasion on which I've talked with him. Once, in the early seventies, he came to the old CBC Radio building on Jarvis Street. As the tape rolled, I said, among other things, "Did you ever think, Prime Minister, that if the War Measures Act had been brought down when you were the young activist law professor I wrote about in *Maclean's, you* might have been arrested?"

"Perhaps," he said. "But I wouldn't have bitched about it."

What style he had! Not only in the way he dressed (remember the ascots, the leather overcoat, the jauntily tilted headgear?) or even in the show-offish athletic behaviour, the pirouettes and the back flips (or, unforgettably, the slide down the royal banister in London). Not even in the arrogance of the "fuddle-duddle" (yeah, sure, Prime Minister) or "just watch me," or the upraised finger to the world. While all those things may have set him apart it was, surely, the sheer power of his *intellect* that made us hold him in awe. Over the years, I've had the privilege of interviewing every Canadian prime minister from Pearson to Chrétien, though not always when they were in office. All those occasions were challenging and memorable. But Trudeau was a breed apart. As someone said about Bobby Orr, when he was the dominant hockey player in the NHL, "He ought to play in a higher league."

As I sit watching him this evening, my mind goes back to one of our last interviews. It was in a suite at the Ritz Carlton hotel in Montreal. Before I could even frame my first question, he began to recite, as if to himself, "I grow old . . . I grow old . . . I shall wear the bottoms of my trousers rolled." I thought then, as I think now, could any other prime minister ever have begun an interview by quoting T. S. Eliot?

The evening in Toronto, to mark the first English-language publication of *Cité Libre*, the magazine of ideas he helped to found in the fifties, drones on. Too many speakers, too many words. For all the spirit of celebration, there is an overtone of sadness in the air. Almost everyone in the crowd is over fifty, and many of the dreams they shared so long ago have been dashed by the tides of history. Looking around, in fact, I wonder where else in the country he could still draw such a crowd. Not in the West, surely, and certainly not in his own Quebec, where, by 1995, he had grown so unpopular that organizers of the referendum's No campaign kept him under wraps.

Trudeau himself doesn't take the podium. He is feeling his age, he has said; his memory is uncertain. But ours isn't, is it? I wonder, as I watch him, if we'll ever see his like again.

PART TWO

Moments

If You Really Want to Hear About It . . .

When ARLENE PERLY RAE, who is an ardent crusader for literacy and children's books as well as the wife of one of Ontario's several living former premiers, asked me to write up a little something for a project she's been working on, I had only one condition. Her project will be a book about books*— various people's reminiscences of works they read as children or teenagers which, as Arlene wrote to her potential collaborators, "woke you up, stirred your soul or changed your life"— and my condition was that I get to write about J. D. Salinger's *The Catcher in the Rye*, which had done all of that (and more) for me when I'd first read it, and which, because I

---

* Arlene's book, *Everybody's Favourites*, was published by Viking in 1997. The paperback edition was scheduled for August 1998.

figured a lot of people would feel the same about it, I wanted to get first dibs on.

I've always had a special feeling for *The Catcher in the Rye*. I was seventeen when it was published, just a year or so older, as I recalled, than Holden Caulfield, its protagonist and narrator, and I was just finishing up at a boarding school in Ontario that bore a lot of resemblance to the prep school in Pennsylvania where he was going — except, of course, Holden runs away in the book and I never did, although, to tell you the truth, I thought about it a couple of times. Books had been part of my life as long as I could remember — my librarian mother had made sure I knew Winnie-the-Pooh and Dr. Dolittle before I could throw a ball — but nothing had ever hit me the way Holden and his tale did. Right from the opening words ("If you really want to hear about it . . ."), I found something I had never found before: someone on the printed page who was of my age, who thought the same things were funny as I did, and the same things crazy, and who said aloud (or in writing) things I could only imagine. It changed forever the way I thought about school, about honesty, about families — I longed for someone in my life like Holden's sister, Phoebe — and about books and the people who wrote them, and in every way, it seemed to me, it fit the criteria Arlene was looking for.

I had, however, a couple of small problems. One was that I was still slightly troubled by the fact that I'd chosen an American book. Over the years, the work I do has put me into the middle of what we now realize has been the golden age of CanLit, and I've spent too much of my life in the world of Canadian writers and writing not to want to push them any time I get a chance. Furthermore, dozens of those writers — heck, hundreds — from W. O. Mitchell to Mordecai Richler, from Alice Munro to Dennis T. Patrick Sears (the author of a little masterpiece called *The Lark in the Clear Air*), and so many other Canadians have been important to me in ways that even Salinger was not. But *The Catcher in the Rye* was the book of my adolescence, and this time, I figured, I could leave my cultural chauvinism in the drawer.

My other problem was more practical. As I sat down to write, I realized I didn't have a copy of the book, and I needed to look up such matters as Holden's exact age and the name of his school. Well, I thought, I'll just amble down to the local library, which I use all the time and whose environs, not only because they remind me of my mother, I always enjoy.

The librarians were busy. I ventured an encounter with the computer. To my surprise, I found both J. D. Salinger and his masterwork with no difficulty. But the copy in my village had been checked out a year ago and the one down the road, in Pefferlaw, was simply "lost."

"This happens all the time," a librarian said when she became free. "Books on the school reading lists are taken out and never returned."

"Nuts," I said, explaining what I wanted it for.

"Well, we do have the Coles Notes," said the librarian.

"Coles *Notes*?" I said. "I'm a serious man of literature. I can't be seen leaving here with . . . "

"Use it here," she said, bringing forth a copy.

"I . . . well . . . I . . . , " I said, and opened the familiar yellow-and-black-striped binding at the list of characters. Hmm. Holden was sixteen, just as I remembered. The school? Pencey. In Agerstown, Pa. And . . .

"And do you do *all* your writing with Coles Notes?" said the man next to me at the counter, laughing.

"Sure I do," I said. "They're Canadian, aren't they?"

Putting the Play Back in Games

A WAVE BREAKS over my bathing suit, cold but exhilarating. I cup my hands and splash my hair and face. Another breaker heads for my midriff. I link my thumbs over my head and count to three. One . . . two . . . well, maybe in a moment. I lower my arms and hug myself, rubbing my biceps, such as they are, and the goose pimples of my chest. *Ooooeee*, it's cold. Another wave approaches. This is it, I think. One . . . two . . . I raise my arms again and — this *is* it — hurl myself headlong into the oncoming swell. *Aaaaahhh.*

I glide like a seal under the waves, kicking gently to keep the momentum. I loose my thumbs and press the backs of my hands together, break into an underwater breaststroke, open my eyes to watch the pebbles sliding under my prow and then, in a rush of exaltation, burst the surface. The whitecaps sparkle as I brush the water from my eyes. I bellyflop into the waves again, try a few strokes of what would be an Australian crawl if I could ever smooth it out, flip halfway over and dog-paddle on my side, roll to my back and flail the air, close my eyes and hold my breath as I tumble in the rolling current, then reach for the stony bottom with my feet and rise once more to gulp the summer air. I'm refreshed and happy. I'm *playing*. And I'm far, far from the world of what, I'm afraid, we have come to think of as sport.

I don't know when games turned grim, or were taken over by people who appear to have just arrived from another galaxy. As the novelist Dan Jenkins has written (approximately), "I liked baseball OK before the players all wore leotards and were paid $16 million a year for scratching themselves." But it's not only baseball. *Every* sport you see on TV has long ago lost any resemblance to the games real people play: football with its hooded behemoths (and diagrams with enough Xs and Os to plot the reinvasion of Normandy), basketball with its leaping freaks (a *small* forward is now usually about six foot eight), even hockey, which has somehow turned from the joyous game of our young lives into a grinding, pounding, shoot-the-puck-into-the-corner exhibition of determination over skill. None of them are any *fun* any more. The Olympics? I yield to no one in my admiration of the achievements and the spectacle. And yes, I confess, I watch every glorious minute. But the athletes as extensions of ourselves? Let's just say real people swim the way I do; Olympians shave their body hair.

The best example I know of, though, is golf. Professional

golfers simply don't play the same game my friends and I do. For one thing, they don't get to hit the ball nearly as often, which is what you're out there to do, isn't it? For another, they're far too hard on themselves. They never give each other putts, for example. They stand over little eighteen-inchers for about twenty minutes, quaking and shaking and slowing down the round, whereas my cousin Jack would just say (my cousin Jack had *better* say, since I have just done the same for him), "Heck, Peter, pick it up." And though they don't seem to get nearly as many tricky lies as my friends and I do, they don't know how to get out of them. Just give it a little kick, we believe, or pick it up to make sure it's yours and then, presto, your lie improves when you put it back down.

Pros don't even take mulligans. A mulligan, in case the only golf you know is the kind on television, is a privilege you negotiate with your fellow players before the round begins. It allows you to disregard your worst shot and hit it again without penalty. Knowing when to use a mulligan is a crucial part of our game and, we're convinced, makes it more pleasant to play. But not those guys. On the rare occasions they hit the kind of shot we hit all the time, they just shake their heads and traipse off into the woods — although I do notice they're clever enough to line the fairways with crowds of people whose shins act like pool-table bumpers and bounce their errant drives back onto the short grass.

No wonder they never smile, eh? They should all take their Day-Glo trousers off and come for a swim.

And the Games Back in Play

MY COUSIN JACK INVENTED Indoor Trivial Bocce one evening last summer. We had been playing — well, sort of playing — real bocce outdoors: you know, the Italian equivalent of lawn bowling. Unlike more serious competitors, in fact, whose courts are built of sand or gravel, we actually play on grass. We just kind of throw the pallino (the little target ball) past the lawn chairs and then see who can come closest with their bowls. You score it like curling, the difference being the target — the pallino — moves if you hit it.

"And so," said Jack, after the dinner dishes had been stacked, "we'll spread this blanket on the floor, and I'll get some marbles from the —"

Our family is a little games-whacky. There are more games

at our grandparents' old cottage — where Jack now reigns — than you can shake a Ping-Pong paddle at: Chinese checkers, Monopoly, Pictionary, crokinole. There are cribbage boards and a mah-jongg set and enough playing cards — including some miniature decks my grandmother used to use for a game that she called Poker Patience — to stock a bridge cruise. But the heart of our recreational life has always been the dart board on the verandah. We've played there ever since Jack's father, my uncle Ernest, came back from the war, sporting an English pub certificate for scoring three triple twenties. And it's at the dart board that Jack, who has inherited his father's eye, invented his masterpiece: *Trivial Darts*.

Trivial Darts — I'll try to keep this simple — is based on the old game called Round the Clock, in which the players must shoot all the numbers on the board in order. First one to twenty wins. In Trivial Darts, though, you can't count your number unless you also answer a question from Trivial Pursuit. Miss the question and you have to hit the number again. Smart, eh? We often play in teams, with one designated shooter, and the rest combining for the questions.

So now, I'm sure, you'll understand Indoor Trivial Bocce. The marbles Jack had found, large and hefty, were from a game — I'd forgotten about this one — called Abalone. One team would have four of the black ones; the other, four of the white. "And this golf ball," he explained, "will be the pallino. The team that's closest to it gets to answer one question; if two of yours are inside your closest opponent's, you get two — and so on to a maximum of four. You get points only for correct answers. First team to, oh, say, eleven, wins."

Too complicated? In case you don't have a cousin Jack, here's as simple and elegant a game as I know. I don't know who invented it. My son Mick brought it from Vancouver a couple of Christmases ago and he called it Name Droppers.

All you need are some pencils, lots of small pieces of paper and a watch with a second hand. You play in pairs, and, yes, couples, married or otherwise, are allowed. To begin, each player (the more the merrier) writes names of well-known people, living, dead — even fictional — on the slips of paper, one to a slip. Do lots: ten or twenty each. Then throw all the names into a hat. As each player's turn comes round, he (or she) starts drawing names. The object is to convey each one to your partner. The only real rule is you can't say the name itself — or spell it. Almost anything else is allowed: rhymes, descriptions, analogies. To get, say, Silken Laumann, you could do anything from "First name sounds like it's made of cloth, second name rhymes with ploughman," to "The champion rower who hurt her leg." Preston Manning? "He isn't 'womaning,' he's . . ." Got it? The object is *speed*— the winners of each round are the team that gets the most names in its pair of two-minute turns — and you'd be surprised how easy it is to mess up. I remember someone missing Bob Dylan once, for example, when his partner struggled to conjure up Dylan Thomas ("He wrote 'Blowin' in the Wind' " would probably have done it), and one relationship started to crumble when a possible fiancée couldn't come up with Bill Vander Zalm from "the B.C. premier who owned Fantasy Gardens."

Anyway, give it a try. You'll have fun. If it doesn't work, I'll send Jack around. I think he's working on combining Name Droppers with Parcheesi.

And Even, Sometimes, Lying

AT ONE TIME OR ANOTHER over the years, I have lifted Karen Kain to my shoulder and kept her there, scored a goal on Andy Moog with an assist from Wayne Gretzky and played one of the greatest chess masters in history to a draw. Am I boasting? You betcha. But am I lying? Well, yes. But only once, and the point of all this is for you to figure out about what.

This is all part of a game we used to play on Morningside, the CBC Radio program I was lucky enough to host for fifteen happy years. We stole our game unabashedly from a French-language TV show, and named it Lie Detector. After we started playing, I heard from a few people who said they used to play something like it in their living rooms. And if it isn't a family game, I figured, it ought to be.

We played three-handed, with a fourth person as a kind of traffic cop. To begin, one player would make, as I have at the beginning here, three boastful statements: two true, one a lie. Then, for a limited time — we allowed a minute and a half — each of the other players would cross-examine the storyteller. When they'd both finished the questioning, they'd each have to guess which was the lie. One point for ferreting it out, one for the fibber for each wrong guess. Then the second player would tell three tales, and so on. Pretty simple, eh? How would you do against me?

Did I really lift Karen Kain? Yup, live on television, sometime in the 1970s. Karen was a guest on 90 Minutes Live, the late-night show I used to host (and which I don't miss at all, by the way), and to show how agile and athletic she was, she stood, in a tutu, in front of me. I placed my trembling hands on her slim, elegant waist and bent at the knees to give her as much hoist as I could muster. She leaped. Miraculously, she rose in the air as if lifted by some supernatural force and lit on my shoulder as softly as a falling petal. I turned to the camera, holding her aloft like Mark Messier with the Stanley Cup, except my sense of accomplishment, unlike Mark's, was overwhelmed by unmitigated relief.

True? Well, if it is, one of the following isn't:

Edmonton, early 1981. I am writing a book on hockey and as a framework have been following the (then) promising Edmonton Oilers and their rising young superstar, Wayne Gretzky. Although I've had my picture taken at training camp, posed as if for a bubble gum card, wearing Dave Semenko's sweater and holding Dave Lumley's stick as if I know what I'm doing, and, on another occasion, have been allowed to act as stick boy in the Montreal Forum, I am still not part of the team. Now, though, as the Oilers close in on the playoffs, their coach and general manager, Glen Sather, seeks some relief from the tension. After a brisk but short practice at Northlands Coliseum, he declares an open session of old-fashioned shinny and, to my astonishment, says, "Wanna play, Zosk?" "Are you kidding?" I reply. I borrow a stick and suit up.

And here I am. Gretzky at centre, Glenn Anderson on left wing, me on the right. The puck is a tennis ball, just as in all our youths, the body checking is (thank heavens) nonexistent, and the speed of the game, if not all the participants, is supersonic. Ron Low is in our goal, Andy Moog in the other. Suddenly, the tennis ball goes behind the net — Gretzky's office, as the players say. I lumber awkwardly to the edge of the crease. Wayne digs it out, flips it right onto the blade of my stick and, bingo, I have a memory for a lifetime.

But if *that's* true, and if I really did lift Karen Kain, then I must be lying about playing to a draw with a grand master of chess, eh? But I did that — live, on the radio; scores of thousands of people heard me. We played in our heads, too, not deigning to use a board. The grand master was the Russian Boris Spassky and — oh, sorry, you're out of time for cross-examination.

So which one is my lie? Well, I really did lift Karen Kain — it really was magical — and, honestly, I had a draw with Spassky.

It was on Morningside. I moved P-K4; he moved P-K4 (the most common of chess openings). As a joke, I offered him a draw. Getting it, and being a gentleman, he accepted.

I played shinny with Wayne and his teammates, too. But when he passed the ball out in front of the net, I flubbed it entirely, and the only way I can claim to have scored with an assist from him is to lie, as I've just done, through my teeth. Makes a good game, though, don't you think?

A Heck of a Guy, Remembered

IN SUMMER, WHEN LAKE ONTARIO laps the shoreline and the sun plays over the mown grass, few people who use the park — families mostly, with kids throwing a Frisbee or kicking a soccer ball around, and young couples walking hand in hand across the lawn — ever give much thought to who it's named for. The monument at its centre, heaven knows, is scarcely prepossessing: a steel-and-concrete "teepee," open at the sides, with its peak chopped off and a strange green spike, not unlike that of an old Prussian helmet, perched on top. For anyone who is curious, though — and who has missed or been confused by the modest sign at the highway's edge — the identity of the man the park's name honours and a brief outline of his accomplishments are spelled out in the teepee's open interior.

A bronze bust of his handsome (if I may say so) mutton-chopped visage, mounted on a concrete pedestal, stares inward from the lake toward the skyline of Toronto's west end, where, until almost exactly a century ago, he lived.

The bust is of, and the park is named for, Sir Casimir Stanislaus Gzowski, my own great-great-grandfather, an important figure of nineteenth-century Canada and (if I may say so again) a heck of a guy. He was born in Poland in 1813, the son of a nobleman, educated as an engineer, swept up in a rebellion against the Russian occupying forces, captured, exiled, called to the American bar (he had, curiously, studied law to learn English), employed on the Erie Canal and sent to Canada on business. He settled here (I am condensing what ought to be a book) and rose to eminence, building everything from bridges (the first over the Niagara River), to railways (much of the Grand Trunk), to a tradition of thoroughbred horse-racing (he effectively launched the Queen's Plate). In 1879 Queen Victoria named him her Canadian aide-de-camp, and in 1890 knighted him.

My family and I, as I'm sure you can tell, are very proud of his memory, even though, in spite of our name, his genes are a fraction of ours. (I'm one-sixteenth Polish, for example; my kids just one thirty-second.) And earlier this year, when the Polish-Canadian community arranged to have the Nobel Peace Prize winner and former Polish president Lech Walesa lay a wreath at Gzowski Park during his brief visit to Canada, we accepted with honour and enthusiasm an invitation to be, so to speak, there with them both — two men from different centuries who had fought, each in his own way, to rid their country of tyranny.

The park was very different from the way it is in summer. For one thing, everyone who was there knew not only who the park was named for but nearly all the reasons why. There were, perhaps, a hundred people there, and all of them, I'm sure — except perhaps for the security men wearing hearing aids and talking into their shirt-sleeves — were of Polish extraction, even the scouts and guides who lined the path to the monument. For another, it was really cold, as only Toronto gets when the winds swirl in from the lake.

And now, Lech Walesa was late. Not much, and no one could blame him — he had a ferocious schedule — but, still, late, and we were freezing.

Finally, the limousines arrived. Walesa debarked, a dapper figure in a blue suit, shrugging into the lightest of Burberry coats to shield himself from the Canadian winds. We met and shook hands, speaking through his interpreter, then walked together between the lines of blue-kneed scouts and guides. In person, I could not help thinking, he looked a lot like the pictures I've seen of Sir Casimir: clear skin, drooping white moustache, aquiline nose and a steadfast expression. As we walked toward the monument, he spoke to one of the dignitaries in Polish. I strained to eavesdrop. He seemed to be discussing the weather, though the only word I could make out clearly was, I think, *Siberia.*

We huddled before the monument. He laid his wreath, spoke briefly and extemporaneously with me. I thanked him for his remarks about my distinguished ancestor. He smiled, said it was too cold for formal addresses, took from his pocket two typewritten pages, signed one, handed it to me, shook hands again and left for his next appointment.

Standing in the blustery wind, with Lech Walesa's autograph in my pocket and the bust of my great-great grandfather towering over my head — in life, he was six foot five — I thought of what a country Sir Casimir helped to build, and now, when summer has returned and the families frolic in the sun, I think of, and am grateful for, the way our heroes are folded into how we live.

When You've Met One Goodyear . . .

AS SOON AS THE CALL CAME THROUGH, I knew it couldn't be good news. We were less than four hours from curtain time — if, that is, we could raise the curtain on cue — and we were having, shall we say, problems.

Rehearsals and sound checks were nearly two hours behind. Karen Kain, who had graciously given up her day off from the National Ballet of Canada to do *The Dying Swan* for us (it had taken two extra stagehands four hours to lay a special floor), needed to get away for a crucial pre-show massage. The truck with our exquisite programs had gone to the wrong address. One of the flats we had borrowed wouldn't fit in the freight elevator. The remote microphones Moxy Früvous would use to open the show weren't being picked up by the sound system. The television technician who had solved the riddle of how to magnify Michael Kusugak's intimate Inuit string games for an audience of a thousand had to leave for another engagement. The people around me seemed — astonishingly — to be calm and collected, but I, trying to play Flo Ziegfeld to the literacy movement, had the heebie-jeebies.

"It's a Mrs. Davey," said Shelley Ambrose, my unquenchable assistant, handing me the phone. "She says she won't talk to anyone but you."

I think this may have been Gill's idea — you know, Gill Howard, with whom I live. Over the years, she's seen the golf tournaments we started in 1986 spread right across the country. Now there's one in every province and one in each territory, all raising money for literacy, and nearly all of them, it sometimes seems, have picked up on the idea that started at the Briars, in Ontario, when the party Gill and I used to host the evening before the golf grew too big for our house, and we moved everything down the road to the Red Barn theatre and threw a kind of informal concert.

So last summer, Gill said, "Why don't we bring everything together in the spring and stage a huge concert at the Winter Garden Theatre in Toronto?" And now here we were. March 1. Certainly the biggest event we'd ever undertaken.

"I'm afraid," said Mrs. Davey, who turned out to be Oscar Peterson's version of Shelley, "that Oscar won't be able to make it tonight. He's been having vision problems — he's at the doctor's now — and it's not only that he couldn't play, he couldn't navigate. We're very sorry."

I knew Oscar Peterson, who is as fine a gentleman as he is a musician, wouldn't take such a decision lightly and I asked Mrs. Davey to please pass on to him my sympathies and my hopes for a speedy recovery.

Still, my heart sank. Our lineup was studded with outstanding Canadian performers — Murray McLauchlan, Prairie Oyster, Tom Jackson, Mordecai Richler, Roch Carrier, Cynthia Dale, Rebecca Jenkins, and Sheila McCarthy, to add but a few to those I've already mentioned. But somehow Oscar Peterson, the greatest jazz piano player in the world, had been the jewel in our diadem, and it was his name, which topped the long list on all our advertising, that had been crucial in signing up a number of corporate sponsors — including, I'm happy to report, the publishers of *Canadian Living* — and helped to sell out the Winter Garden for as much as $200 a seat.

Three hours to show time. We racked our collective brains. Could we fly Oliver Jones in from Montreal? Too late. Book a great classical pianist? None available. And then Louise Wood, the bright and indefatigable young woman we'd hired to pull everything together, said, "Stewart Goodyear — that wonderful young pianist everyone's talking about. He's just fifteen now, but he's been playing all kinds of concerts. You had him on Morningside, in fact, on a panel of prodigies. Besides, he lives in Toronto."

"Perfect," I barked. No one could replace Oscar Peterson. But a kid might just —

I sprang into action.

"Someone get me the Goodyear number from Morningside," I yelled. "Someone else get his agent on the phone."

Moments later, I had the agent on the line. "Hi," I said. "This is Peter Gzowski —"

"Oh, hi, Peter. Nice to hear from you."

"— and I have an incredible request for Stewart. It's for tonight, and —"

"You mean Scott, don't you?" he said.

"Yes, whatever," I said. Louise must have misremembered the name. I understood. I occasionally do that myself under stress. "Anyway, Oscar Peterson has had to cancel an engagement at the very last moment, and we were wondering if—"

"You know Scott is an Indy driver, eh?"

"Yes, well, sure — uh, sorry," I said. "You don't suppose he could learn to play the piano in a couple of hours, do you?"

Curtain time. Somehow, Louise and Shelley and Nancy Franklin, who usually produces music for the radio but had joined in the throng of volunteers for the Winter Garden, have managed to track Stewart Goodyear down at his high school, talk his mother into letting him do his homework later, and to arrange, miraculously, for him to be here.

The houselights dim, only a few minutes late. Moxy Früvous come prancing down the aisle, their mikes working perfectly. Karen has had her massage. The programs have arrived. I know, at last, the evening will work. It is, after all, now out of my hands.

The Day We Bought the Sheep

THE SHEEP WAS LOT NO. 31, two down from the piece we'd really been sticking around for — and had, somewhat to my surprise (and for quite a bit more money than I'd ever intended to bid), happily acquired. Besides, as Gill reminded me now, we'd already splurged in the silent auction that had opened the afternoon, picking up a nifty pair of costume earrings donated by a local craftsperson and, for a cool twenty dollars, *fifty* dollars worth of haircuts from Lisa, who runs the Mane Idea on the village's main street.

But the sheep was . . . well, the sheep, and, as Gill was the first to say, the perfect answer to her perennial Christmas problem: a gift for her hugely successful litigation-lawyer brother Peter, a man who really does have everything, including a whacky sense of office design.

We decided to stick around.

I don't know when people first decided to use auctions for good causes. Years ago, the only sales I ever knew about — or went to — were on the lawns of old farmhouses. You went there to look for pine furniture, trying to outwit the steely-eyed professionals on painted-over chests-of-drawers, or searching for bargains among the tinted tumblers and the sturdy iron pans.

Those sales still go on, I'm sure. I imagine the pickings are getting slimmer, though, and in some cases — I'm thinking of all those dying prairie towns — there's more sadness than shopping in the air. But in my world at least, auctions have changed. They feature new stuff, not old, and the money they raise goes not to tidy up someone's estate but to help some charity or worthy institution survive.

I see this all the time. All over the country, the golf tournaments we hold for literacy are looking for new ways to sweeten the pot. A lot of them have turned to auctions. We've sold Rita MacNeil's hat in Dartmouth, Nova Scotia, and a Christopher Pratt print in St. John's, Newfoundland, golf bags in Victoria and symphony tickets in Ottawa. Once, in the Yukon, someone paid $2,100 to have Cynthia Dale caddy for him (Audrey McLaughlin went for just a little less), and someone else coughed up $650 for her Street Legal jacket. When we gathered with the Assembly of First Nations in Calgary this year, one of the stars of North of 60 bought a new pair of golf shoes for the occasion and, when he found they didn't fit him, put them into the auction — signed — and made nearly as much as he'd paid for them to help support aboriginal languages.

And so on and so on. Our auctions don't always work as well as we'd like. Sometimes, in fact, we see the people who've worked so hard scrounging up the items in the first place desperately bidding just to get some action (I think it was John Savage, then the mayor of Dartmouth, who bought Rita MacNeil's hat), and, I confess, I've picked up an item or two myself I don't really need. But they do make *some* money and, even when they're limping, they're fun.

Now, the day of the sheep, the action is lively.

A couple of hundred of us have gathered at the Red Barn Theatre, just down the road from Gill's and my place at Lake Simcoe, in Ontario. The Red Barn is Canada's oldest professional summer theatre but, in the 1990s, it struggles to stay alive. For most of this season — to judge by what they've assembled — volunteers have been scouring the community. They've drummed up lube jobs and lunches, plane rides and carpet cleanings — and thirty pounds of free-range chickens. Half the neighbourhood seems to have kicked in. Curtis Joseph, the St. Louis Blues goalie who comes from nearby, has sent an autographed stick, and a man with a PhD has volunteered to teach you anything you want for six free hours. Masseurs will massage you, an artist will sketch your house, and Lisa will cut your (or, as it turns out, my) hair. And through the afternoon, it's been as if everyone who *didn't* kick in is determined to buy something donated by someone who did.

Lot No. 29, which I'd had my eye on, was a delicious little painting of the Barn itself, fashioned on hardboard by Mrs. Sheila Ruth Maloney of Zephyr, Ontario, and showing people streaming into the old building while the cows stream out. Unfortunately for my wallet, one of my neighbours had *his* eye on it, too, and, as I say, I paid . . . okay, okay, it was $300. But it *is* a good cause.

And now, the sheep. It's a fake sheep, actually, made of plywood. It was used as a prop on the TV show The Kids in the Hall. It's stupid — and, as Gill has just noted, the ideal gift for Peter, who keeps a plastic goose in his office and has a phone that quacks like a duck.

"Who'll give me fifty dollars?" says the auctioneer.

Gill, a veteran, stays cool.

"Twenty-five? Twenty-five? Do I hear — ?"

"Oh, dear," says Gill as a hand shoots up. "Someone else wants it." She leans forward, clutching our bidding card.

"Merry Christmas, Peter," I think, as I see the determined look in her eye.*

---

* Having told you that Molly Johnson was one of the brides in the piece called "Swallow Point 1: Passages and Places," I should also confess that Peter Howard was one of the grooms. (They married different people.) I'm pretty sure he didn't take his sheep to the wedding.

Making a Fashion Statement

I AM NOT, AS MY FRIENDS will tell you, the world's snazziest dresser.

People who write things about me or put me on their worst-dressed lists (I tied for first in *Toronto Life* magazine last year) tend to count this among my most notable characteristics. If I kept a scrapbook, I'm sure, the phrase "unmade bed" would appear almost as often as comments on my smoking or my sputtering speech. "Shaggy" would be there a lot, too. "Unkempt."

I do not dress badly on purpose. It's just that clothes and I don't seem to get along. Shirts sprout ink stains on their pockets the day after I buy them, and their tails seek daylight every time I put them on. Sweaters unravel. Trousers wrinkle and droop. Cuffs fray. Socks get divorces in my drawers. Though I seldom wear ties or jackets, burns and coffee stains appear on those I do as if by magic, like frost patterns on a winter window. Belt loops dodge my fumbling fingers. Zippers languish at an embarrassing half-mast, and buttons fall from anything I wear like the leaves of an unwatered *Ficus benjamina*.

I am not a pioneer of this sartorial lack of style. At least two of my heroes, in fact, Stephen Leacock and George Grant — though this is not why I admire them — were as carefree with their appearances as I am insouciant about mine.

Leacock, writes his biographer Ralph Curry, sometimes closed his waistcoat with a safety pin, and "wore his [academic] gown with the aplomb of a little boy playing baseball in torn trousers."

One year, Curry tells us, "A class that became particularly fond of him bought him a new robe. He thanked them generously, and thoughtfully wore the gown the next day. But it was not the same; it rustled. When he appeared the second day in his old robe, the class was not surprised. . . ."

George Grant, philosopher, nationalist, guru to a generation, was no Beau Brummell either. "He used the tail of his fraying Oxford gown to wipe the blackboard clean," writes his biographer William Christian. "Inevitably, even the good students were distracted . . . not by speculations about justice and beauty, but by more mundane matters such as the large hole in his shoe, his trailing shirt-tail, or whether the necktie he was using as a belt would serve its intended purpose."

See? Two of the greatest thinkers Canada has ever produced kept the importance of clothes in perspective. Yet when someone like me comes along a few years later (I actually had the pleasure of interviewing Professor Grant a couple of times before he died, and Leacock, who was a friend of my grandfather's, is buried up the road from where I live at Lake Simcoe), others — even friends — make sport of us. Last New Year's, after an evening in which, as is our tradition, we had plied a small circle of good friends with food and drink and conversation, we arranged for everyone to meet at the elegant neighbourhood resort called the Briars for — again a tradition — brunch. Without much reflection, I put on my favourite plaid shirt (all right, it's missing a button or two), a Christmas sweater that was already showing a trademark burn hole, some familiar flannels that may have lost their last crease about Thanksgiving and a pair of — well, two; they were *almost* the same colour but they weren't quite a couple — grey wool socks. Showing up last, I was greeted by a ripple of laughter.

"What is it?" I inquired as — oops — a forkful of scrambled eggs tumbled into my rumpled lap.

"Oh, it's just," said Peter Sibbald Brown, wearing his customary tweed jacket and cravat, "that you seem to be making such a . . . fashion statement."

Leacock, in particular, would have understood. I had, in fact, a perfect parallel to his favourite-gown story just last year. In October, I was in St. John's and, as I always do, I dropped in at NONIA, the Newfoundland outport nurses' store on Water Street. NONIA, if they won't mind my saying so, run my kind of store — a crafts outlet that began in the

1920s when women living in the outports made beautiful, durable, hand-knit sweaters to help pay for nursing services. I bought my first one in the seventies, a cable-stitched crew neck I came to call Old Blue and which, along with a pair of jeans (I'm past jeans now), became my standard uniform for hosting This Country in the Morning for almost three years. Last fall, I found Old Blue's descendant, and from the day I bought it I wore it almost constantly — it was soft enough that I could wear it on weekends, without benefit of shirt — till Christmas. When, alas, I shrunk it in the washing machine (another skill I've never mastered) and donned the Christmas present I was soon to brand, my colleagues at Morningside, less understanding, apparently, than Leacock's students, issued a statement of relief: "If you didn't change it soon, we were going to go on strike," they said. "We were just tired of looking at you in the same sweater *every* day."

Ah, well, I thought, at least the new one doesn't rustle.

Things My Father Taught Me: Pasta

MY FATHER LIKED TO COOK spaghetti — or, as he taught me to call it, pasta. Actually, he liked to *say* "pasta," too, and, like a lot of non-Italians, he would dramatize it by cupping his thumb to his fingertips and gesturing over the burbling pot. "*Pasta*," he would say. "*Bellissimo.*"

He brought both his smattering of Italian and his taste for new foods back from the war. He learned a lot overseas. He had some tough times, but when he came back — I think this was true for most veterans — he was more interested in talking about the happy memories: the women he'd romanced (he and my mother were divorced long before he went away), the wines he'd liberated, the friends he'd made for life.

"Pasta," he would say, and start to chop some onions.

To my admiring adolescent eyes, this was an act of rare and

exotic daring. In my mother's house, in Galt (as, I imagine, in most of Canada at that time), spaghetti, when we had it, came in cans — short bits of soggy noodles already mixed in a bland tomato sauce. And now here was my father, the world traveller, making a very different dish from scratch. To the sizzling onions, he'd add ground beef and chopped (and seeded) green peppers, garlic — garlic was practically illegal in Galt — salt, pepper (I don't remember him grinding the pepper, but he may have), tinned tomatoes and (something else I'd never heard of) tinned tomato *paste*. After the sauce had simmered for an hour or so, its odour wafting enticingly through his kitchen, he'd boil some noodl . . . sorry, long strands of firm, fresh pasta, until they were — cupping his hand again —"al dente" (I remember him once actually flinging a piece against the refrigerator door to see if it would stick) and serve them, first drained in a colander, with the now delicious sauce spooned over the centre. Then the crowning touch: grated Parmesan cheese spooned over each serving, which we ate, as he showed us, by twirling each long string in a soup spoon and slurping it down uncut. (Only my uncle Ernest, also just back from Europe, was blasé enough to cut his pasta with a knife, but Ernest, his own man, also cut the kernels off his corn on the cob.)

There were, I realize now, similar scenes in kitchens all over the land. The veterans, their palates changed by their experiences, were ready for culinary adventures. And when the waves of immigration that followed them across the Atlantic from Europe and then, later, rolled in from other continents, brought new and unfamiliar foods and recipes to our shores, the veterans welcomed the change. The Canada of overcooked beef and mashed potatoes (not to mention canned spaghetti) would never be the same.

After his pasta, my father liked to offer a green salad. This, too, was a discovery for me, for I had grown up on salads that were served *before* the main course and were (except perhaps for various slaws) virtually tasteless: bowls of iceberg lettuce, quartered pink tomatoes (although, unless my memory deceives me, *all* tomatoes were redder then than now) and sliced carrots and cucumbers drenched in prepared, usually store-bought, dressings, or mounds of chilled aspic or lime-green Jell-O, scattered with many of the same veggies and, occasionally, fruits.

My father's salads were relatively simple: a few greens, some snipped green onions, cucumber slices, the best tomatoes he could find, a few slivers of red or green peppers. But he would prepare his wooden bowl with tender care, rubbing halved cloves of garlic over its interior against scattered grains of salt, and dress the finished product with olive oil and vinegar and — wonder of wonders — mustard.

He was no chef, and would be embarrassed to be called that now. I remember no herbs, no fancy vinegars, no sauces with lofty French names. I have, in fact, probably all but exhausted his culinary repertoire here. But he liked his food and he opened doors for anyone who cared to share his pleasures. And I, for one, as I begin to chop the onions for a midwinter feast of what is now, for us, a basic pasta — with a fresh green salad to follow — am grateful to him.

How Not to Prepare a Duck

THOUGH HE CAME TO IT late in life, as we know, the Aging Voluptuary likes to cook almost as much as he likes to eat. He is particularly fond of taking recipes from his well-thumbed kitchen library and impressing his children and friends with his adventurous spirit. He has dipped into *Greene on Greens* for corned beef and cabbage in horseradish cream (the cabbage is wilted, with tomatoes and shallots and freshly ground pepper, and the sauce, which includes Dijon mustard, sour cream and lemon juice, is practically a dinner in itself), into Jacques Pepin's *Simple and Healthy Cooking* (do not be put off by its dietarily correct title) for navarin of lamb, into Sarah Leah Chase's *Cold Weather Cooking* for veal stew with peppers and olives, the *Harrowsmith* books for soups and stews and (of course) his *Canadian Living* library for almost anything he wants to tackle. And so on. The Voluptuary thinks, indeed, that any cookbook is worth its cover-price if he finds one recipe to add to his repertoire.

And here he is now, working away. His text is from *The Silver Palate Cookbook*, the volume that came out of New York in 1979 and which, the Voluptuary thinks, may have been singly responsible for the fact that nearly everyone with a kitchen had three-quarters of a bottle of blueberry vinegar on the shelf for a short time in history.

This evening, he has selected Duck with Forty Cloves of Garlic. He loves both. If, as *The Silver Palate Cookbook* claims, "there is no such thing as a little garlic," the Voluptuary is also convinced there is no such thing as too much. He puts garlic in his hamburgers and his stews. He inserts slices into his legs of lamb, which he then smothers in rosemary and Dijon mustard. His salad bowl is redolent of being sprinkled with salt and rubbed with garlic. He has been known to roast a bulb on its own, to *triple* the amount recipes call for and, for one of his favourite breakfast dishes, to sauté slices of garlic with mushrooms and thyme, sprinkling the whole, as he finishes, with lemon juice. The Voluptuary may lead a limited social life but he has never been attacked by a vampire.

He is not so familiar with duck. He still remembers the first time he experienced it, in his Saskatchewan days, when a friend presented him with two small feathered trophies of the hunt, and the woman he was later to marry wept as she plucked them for the oven and probed for buckshot in their flesh. He has since restricted himself to the domestic variety. But even he admits he is better at eating it — he relishes a tea-smoked specialty of his favourite Chinese restaurant — than at cooking it. The last time he prepared it, his children maintain (and there was overhead evidence to support them), he became so engrossed in the vigours of carving that splatters of fat hit the ceiling.

This time, he has vowed, will be different. He will take *care*. He has chopped the heart, neck, gizzard and wing tips of his plump protagonist and browned them in sizzling oil. With the heat reduced, he has added onions and carrots, then chicken stock, thyme, parsley, bay leaf, salt and pepper. A rich aroma rises as he sets the oven for 450°F, separates the garlic and discards the papery skin (no other peeling is required). He stuffs six of the largest cloves into the duck's cavity and arranges the rest around the pan. Now, with the oven down to 375° and the duck roasting away, he starts on the final touches of the sauce.

"Step 7," says *The Silver Palate*, "Strain the broth, discard the solids, and . . ."

With his right hand, the Voluptuary takes the saucepan from the stove. In his left, he holds his colander. He moves to the sink. Slowly, and with exquisite care, thinking of the sherry vinegar and cassis he will add to the finished product, he strains the simmering contents of the saucepan through the —

"Oh, *no*!" he exclaims more loudly than he meant to. And the Aging Voluptuary, chef extraordinaire, stares in dismay as the last of his golden gravy swirls down the drain, while he holds, in the colander, the browned giblets and wasted vegetables.

"You know," he says, as his guests enter the kitchen to see what caused his outburst, "sometimes you should try a recipe once or twice before you decide to serve it."

Or Buy Greens

THE AGING VOLUPTUARY, who cooks, as we know, as much for pleasure as from necessity, tends to shop more like a European than a Canadian: for one meal at a time, usually, for two at the most. Sometimes he plans his menus in advance — a cookbook may inspire him — and when he arrives at the market, he heads straight for the shelves on his list, though he has, he admits, been known to be lured astray. More often he just drifts into his favourite butcher's and waits for the muse to hit him; then, when he has selected his meat, he goes next door to the supermarket to find vegetable accompaniment. In whichever mode, he enjoys his excursions.

And here he is now at the checkout counter, feeling, if truth be told, more than a little pleased with himself. From the bounty of the Ontario summer he has picked a symphony of greens and reds and yellows to set off the fresh lamb chops that caught his eye at the butcher's.

The Voluptuary loves vegetables, and as his cooking skills have improved, he has grown more adventurous in their preparation. He has picked up his ideas from everywhere. From the cookbooks of Jacques Pepin he has learned to roast his beets in foil (an hour and a half at 400°F; peel, slice and toss with salt and pepper, olive oil and red wine vinegar); from his friends and neighbours William Whitehead and Timothy Findley — Bill is to cooking, the Voluptuary thinks, as Tiff is to writing novels — to purée his spinach with a blend of leeks and garlic; from his well-thumbed *Greene on Greens* to slice his rutabagas into cubes the size of poker dice and drench them with butter, honey and fresh black pepper in the pan (a trick, the Voluptuary thinks he may have figured out for himself, that also works with carrots and maple syrup); from Linda Barber, a caterer in Edmonton, to make what he is convinced is the world's best warm salad — leeks, mushrooms and garlic gently sautéed in butter, then poured over butter lettuce and dressed with balsamic vinegar; and from Elizabeth Baird, his idol in all things culinary (Elizabeth's latest opus, with the help, once again, of her colleagues at *Canadian Living*, is called simply *Canadian Living's Best Vegetables*), to grill his peppers — they make an entrancing salad with fennel — add garlic to his broccoli and curry to his cold zucchini soups. He is proud of his accomplishments. He has become, he feels, a master of the veggie patch and he enjoys showing his knowledge off.

Nowhere does he find more opportunities than here at the supermarket. Surrounded by tabloid newspapers (he likes to linger in line long enough to peek at the headlines, purely for amusement, you understand, and to glance admiringly at the racks of *Canadian Living* — if only his fellow shoppers knew), he is ready to explain to whoever will listen how he plans to prepare the evening's feast.

He reaches the head of the line. The cashier, he is pleased to note, is one of his favourite students — ever curious about what he has purchased.

"And this?" she says holding a small, magenta head of radicchio.

He tells her. "An expensive but colourful addition to the salad," he intones. "I use it to —"

RAPPINI, she punches in.

Rejecting the opportunity to pick up his ultra-fashionable lettuce at bargain prices, the Voluptuary, who appreciates the small mark up of supermarkets, deigns to correct her.

"And . . . ?" she says, picking up a leafy bundle of greens, veined in red.

"Why, beet greens. You steam them with —"

"We don't have beet greens," says his acolyte, checking her master list.

"Oh, yes, beet greens," he says. "In Nova Scotia last summer I learned how to prepare them with —"

"Swiss chard? We do have swiss chard."

"Swiss chard?" says the Voluptuary.

"Yes," says the person in the lineup behind him, thumbing a copy of *Canadian Living*.

"Oh," says the Voluptuary, trying not to peek at the magazine. "And how, I wonder, do you cook it?"

Just When You Thought It Was Safe to Drink the Water . . .

I PAUSE IN MY OPENING REMARKS, relishing what I dare to think is friendly laughter, and reach under the podium for the glass of water the organizers have so thoughtfully provided, when, suddenly, it hits me. That's how they got him, isn't it? Andy Boychuk, just after he was elected leader of the Saskatchewan opposition. Speaking, in his case, to a political picnic. Paused. Reached for *his* glass of water. And . . . curtains. One sip and he fell over dead.

Fortunately for Boychuk's memory, his faithful speech writer, Joanne Kilbourn, was in the crowd, and a couple of hundred pages later — and after a lot of intrigue and revelations — she was able to bring his dastardly killer to ground. But why die just to start a detective story? I pass on the water and go on with my speech.

You wouldn't think we'd be so good at writing crime fiction, would you? Not gentle, peace-loving us. But in the last ten years or so — maybe more, since Howard Engel's Benny Cooperman made his debut in 1980, rooting out villainy in the thinly disguised St. Catharines, Ontario, he calls Grantham — there's been a real explosion of whodunits, thrillers and just good, juicy detective yarns in and about Canada. The group I am addressing this evening, in fact, the Crime Writers of Canada, now boasts a membership of almost two hundred, and the characters they've created are often hard to forget.

Joanne Kilbourn is one of my favourites. She's a widow — there's a story in that, too — who, like her creator, a delightful and funny English teacher named Gail Bowen, lives in Regina. Unlike a lot of fictional detectives, Joanne, who has two children, actually gets older with every book (there are four of them now) and lives a life with which, except for its grisly elements, ordinary readers can identify. But I also like Benny Cooperman and his chopped egg sandwiches (on white), Jack Batten's lawyer (I'm not sure if he even has a first name) Crang, Eric Wright's police inspector Charlie Salter, Alison Gordon's feisty sportswriter Kate Henry (though I suspect Kate is growing tired of baseball), all of whom practise their craft in Toronto — though Charlie Salter has had cases as far afield as Winnipeg and Prince Edward Island — and many others who live elsewhere.

It's the elsewhere, indeed, that often appeals to me. Much

as I like crime *fiction*, I'm not all that high on crime, and my reading rooms — I read everywhere — are littered with murder mysteries and police procedurals I've begun, enjoyed — and quit halfway through. Whodunit? Most of the time, who-givesadarn? But I like the zany characters I meet and, especially, the places I get to. I know southern California through Sue Grafton's Kinsey Millhone, for example, Boston through Robert B. Parker's Spenser, Navaho country through Tony Hillerman's Joe Leaphorn and Yorkshire through Reginald Hill's Pascoe and Dalziel, among other places and people. And now, thanks to Canadian writers, I'm getting to more and more places here, as well.

Edward O. Phillips, for instance, has taken me into the drawing rooms of Westmount with his waspish Geoffrey Chadwick; Laurence Gough and his Claire Parker and Jack Willows into the seediest corners of Vancouver; Suzanne North (who won the money to buy the computer she writes on by betting at the racetrack) into the horse country of southern Alberta; L. R. Wright all over the Sunshine Coast of B.C. with her librarian Cassandra Mitchell and Staff Sergeant Karl Alberg (I suspect that Bunny Wright, as everyone calls her, now has people touring Sechelt looking for literary clues the way Alice Munro fans search southwestern Ontario); and Scott Young, of all people, into the high Arctic with his Inuk RCMP inspector Matteesie Kitologitak.

I like them all — and a lot of others, too. If their affection for violence seems a little un-Canadian, well, what the heck.

We play hockey, don't we? You don't build a literature with just Governor General's Awards and epic poems. This stuff is not only fun, it matters. It helps tell us who we are.

But I'm still not drinking that water.

The Joys of Channel Surfing

SOMETIMES, TO MY CONSTERNATION, I get lost. I'll be watching, say, Mary Jo Eustace and Ken Kostick chop-chop-chopping on What's for Dinner?— one of my favourite cooking shows anywhere — when they get ready to throw to a commercial, and I start clicking with my thumb again (I don't think I've seen a whole commercial since about 1992) and I get caught up in a political discussion on CPAC or a good roaring tractor pull on TSN, and by the time I remember to go back to Mary Jo and Kenny, as she calls him (she also teases him about wearing a wig, which he doesn't), I can't remember which channel they were on, let alone how many cloves of garlic are supposed to go into the stew. Ah, well. They'll be back; *everyone* seems to come back in the brave new world of multi-channel TV, when things get shown not only all over the dial but over and over again. Sometimes I start watching a hockey game in the evening, turn it off to go to bed early, and then, when I wake — and being careful not to hit one of the channels that might give me the final score — just pick it up again where I left off. Meantime, I wonder, click, click, how Mary Tyler Moore is getting along on channel . . . uh, channel . . . where *is* she, anyway?

All men do this — or so we're told. It's as if using a TV guide and actually *planning* what you're going to watch is like stopping your car to ask for directions when you're lost, which women do but we don't. With the TV remote, instead of thinking ahead, we hop all over the place, sampling here — "Let me just catch the score of the game and we can come back to Masterpiece Theater"— skipping there, driving whoever's sitting with us to distraction. But I'm worse than most, I'm pretty sure, partly because of my weird hours. In the spring of 1997, I finally stepped down after fifteen years in the lovely job on CBC Radio whose single unlovely aspect was that I had to get up at three o'clock in the morning to do it. But my body hasn't yet figured out that we've changed our schedule. It still nudges me awake when sensible people are sleeping, and, click, there I go, prowling the flickering channels of pre-matitudinal TV.

It's a strange and surprisingly busy world. In it, people applaud when the guy in the infomercial tries unsuccessfully to set fire to his car wax. They jump up and down when someone says something especially stupid on one of the endless parade of tasteless talk shows — Jerry Springer, say.

Others with sleek bodies and not many clothes twist themselves pretzel-like onto contraptions that rock on the floor and, presumably, give you abs (whatever they are) like a washboard, or murmur their 900 numbers as they boogie, in the hopes, apparently, that I will interrupt my nocturnal channel-surfing and give them a call (at about $3.95 a minute) to ease their loneliness.

There are spicy moments, too, on the movie channels if you have them, and occasionally on Bravo! or Showcase or one of those naughty French stations. It's pretty tame stuff, from what I've (blush) seen, though I'm bemused by the regulation that makes the broadcasters put warnings on it. I picture some innocent teenager, whose life would be ruined if he so much as caught a glimpse of a bare pink bosom (though he's apparently fine watching people get their heads lopped off in prime time), clicking through the dial just like me. He comes across a note about the raciness of what's coming up. Do the regulators really think that he — or, for that matter, I — would react by saying, "Oh, my goodness, nudity! I'd better turn away from *that*!"

For all the drivel and the exploitation, though, and all the commerce and the banality — and yes, much of it is a vast wasteland — there's a *life* to television when you click your way around it. You never know when you're going to find a new stand-up comic or see a profile of Picasso or watch a really silly quiz game or drop in on a lyrical ballet or catch — perhaps especially on the Discovery Channel — a glimpse of a world you'd have never seen otherwise.

Or maybe just come across something as relaxed and pleasant to watch as What's for Dinner? Who knows, you might even learn something — especially if when you cook you have someone who measures all the ingredients into those neat little glass bowls first.

That is, of course, if you can remember what channel it was on.

Notes of a Driver Whose Car Is Smarter than He Is

I'LL BE OFF TO THE ARCTIC again about the time you read this, but I still think it's safe to assume — it is, isn't it?— that the threat of winter has passed by now and I can talk about something that happened during the coldest of times without running the risk of bringing them back.

Man, it was cold, eh?— except in Vancouver where, as I remember, the rhododendrons started to come out in January. Everywhere else, pipes froze, people froze, the world froze. But maybe if I hadn't scratched The Car in the first place, I'd . . .

You remember The Car, don't you? It's the sleek black beauty I couldn't afford but splurged on anyway after I was seduced by a luxurious drive down some country roads. It intimidated me, as I said then, and I didn't feel comfortable in it until, on its maiden voyage, I backed into the garbage box at the foot of our driveway and gouged a long, ugly scratch on its left rear fender, sort of putting my stamp on it. Three days later, and just after I'd written that first column, I put a matching scar on the *right* rear fender, using a fire hydrant in Toronto. And not long after that, while I was backing into an underground parking spot, I ran the aerial into a concrete ledge and all but lost my FM.

I don't do these things on purpose, you know. I'm actually a careful driver. I just wasn't made to drive expensive cars.

Or, I guess, park them. In spite of the warnings of the salesman who'd delivered it to me in the first place, I kept leaving the car under the ailing tree in our front yard. Drop by drop over the summer, the poor, tired tree oozed a sickly white liquid over The Car's gleaming surface. By fall, as I've written elsewhere, it looked as if a squadron of Stuka dive-pigeons had used it for target practice.

Since The Car is of a breed whose company prides itself on its service, of course — including a luxurious wash and polish every time you take it in — a normal owner, even if he'd treated his vehicle as badly as I had, would have fixed these things up as they occurred.

Not me. The worse things got, the more reluctant I grew to let the people who'd sold it to me see it. I was embarrassed. I drove right through its 6,000-kilometre checkup, its 12,000, its — I just kept driving; if my route ever threatened to take me near the dealer's, I went blocks out of my way.

Was I, for all that, enjoying the luxury?

Sort of, to be honest. Whatever you do to its exterior, The Car runs like a mirage; it fairly *purrs* along on the highway while its radio (even with the aerial askew) bathes you in soft music; it takes curves like a cloud; it stops on a loonie and, in winter, if you press a little button, it warms your bum.

Still, there were times when I wondered if paying more than I should have hadn't bought me less than I wanted. It was like the time, years ago, when I needed to gussy up my wardrobe for television; I discovered that if I paid enough for a shirt, it wouldn't have a breast pocket. Or the fact that it costs more to have an unlisted number than a listed one. With The Car, it was fancy push-button windows — which are harder to open in winter than the ones you have to crank.

But now here we were, Gill and I, pulling out of the driveway in the midst of one of the winter's coldest snaps. We were off to dinner with some friends.

Except that The Car was sort of rumbling and was a bit hard to steer. "I think," said Gill, "you have a flat tire."

"Too cold to stop," I said. We rumbled ahead to a roadside restaurant and pulled into the parking lot. Gill was right. Actually, doubly right. There were *two* flat tires. We abandoned ship. "I don't think you can change them anyway," Gill said. "That fancy doohickey they gave you is back at home — you know, the trick lock that means that no one can steal your hubcaps."

"——," I said. We called a friend. Only an hour and a half late, we arrived at dinner, chagrined. "But I thought you drove an expensive car," said our host. "How could *its* tires have gone flat in the cold?"

A week later — a week I spent without a car at all — I could have answered him.

"You want me to be honest?" said the mechanic who finally fixed my tires. "You haven't taken it in for its regular maintenance, have you?"

"Well, er . . ."

"While you've been driving, the tires have been getting softer and softer. These are very good tires, you know — they can handle 170 miles an hour. But in the cold, when they're soft anyway, they separate from the rims. You drove right out of them."

"Ah," I said. "It's probably time to get those scratches fixed anyway."

And Who Loses Things

ALTHOUGH I WAS NEVER much of a fan of the old TV show Candid Camera — I used to feel sorry for the people who fell into their traps and wonder how, other than looking stupid, they were *expected* to behave — there are still some scenes from it that stick in my mind. In one, a man comes into a bakery, the only customer. The baker, nevertheless, says, "Take a number." The customer takes from the peg, as I recall, fifty four. The baker starts calling his list, beginning at about thirty-five. "Thirty-six, thirty-seven, thirty-eight . . ." The man looks perplexed but says nothing. "Thirty-nine, forty, forty-one." Still no response. The count speeds up. "Forty-six, forty-seven, forty-eight." Faster and faster. "Fifty-one, fifty-two." A blur now. "Fifty-three, fifty-four, fifty-five, fifty-six . . ."

"Excuse me," says the customer.

"Sorry, sir," says the baker, "you've missed your turn."

The man, of course, looks stupid.

I'm replaying the scene now, standing in a large room on the second floor of a huge Orwellian Ontario government building. I wouldn't be here in the first place if I didn't lose things. I don't know when this started. Maybe it's a function of age. I know I'm sometimes absent-minded now, like the professor in all those stories. ("Which way was I walking when we met?" "Towards the physics building, sir." "Good, then I've had my lunch.") I ride past my floor in the elevator dreaming of other worlds, and leave home — or try to — without my car keys. Sometimes, when I'm wandering around the office in the morning, I lose my half-finished cup of coffee — or, worse, my notes for the upcoming program. I just leave them somewhere and can't remember where. The people who work in the control room when I'm on the radio have long since learned to keep extra copies of my briefing notes, so that when they see me groping frantically among my papers they can rush in with a backup before the next guest arrives.

Once, I couldn't find my glasses, and was about to panic until someone pointed out they were just where I'd left them, pushed up on my forehead. It's a miracle I still have my wallet, having left it, as I have, everywhere from restaurants in Toronto to the airport washroom in Yellowknife.

This time it's my birth certificate. I don't know *where* I've put it, and even Gill, who can usually find anything I've lost, is baffled. I need it — and quickly — for a passport. By the time I realized it was missing — I looked all over for it, as they say in Newfoundland, and there it was, gone — Gill and I were practically due to leave the country for a long-planned vacation (well, sort of long-planned). There was no solution but to go get a new one. And here I am. I have, with some difficulty, found the bureau I'm looking for and have joined the line that snakes in from the door. When I reach the front, the receptionist looks over the form I've filled out and gives me a number: three hundred thirty-five.

"Area B," she says. "They'll call you."

I have, it turns out, lined up to line up.

There's something else, too. I'm not happy here. I don't like large, anonymous offices. I react to all fortresses of bureaucracy the way Stephen Leacock did to banks: When I go into them I get rattled. I'm rattled now. On the form in my hand, I've written my father's name wrong and mixed up the day and month of my own birthday. I've fixed it up, but I know I'll lose marks for, if nothing else, neatness.

I move to Area B and look at the number they're working on now. Three hundred nineteen. Visions of bakeries dance in my head.

I sit and open my briefcase, looking for something to read.

"Three twenty," a clerk calls from behind the counter. There's nothing to read in my briefcase except an old Visa bill and two letters I have — darn — forgotten to mail. It seems an hour before I hear "Three twenty-one." It's ten minutes.

"Three twenty-eight, three twenty-nine, three thirty . . ."

Is it my imagination, or is she going faster?

"Three thirty-three, three thirty-four . . ."

I rise. I haven't closed my briefcase. The contents spill on the floor: Visa bill, unmailed letters, extra ID, pencils.

"Three thirty-five," I hear from behind the counter.

"Wait," I fairly shout. "Wait for me."

"Of course, sir," says the clerk. "Take your time."

As I bend to repack my briefcase, I think that maybe I should add to the list of things I forget old television shows. Still, like the man in the bakery, I'm feeling — and probably looking — pretty stupid.

Including (Occasionally) His Glasses

I SCRAMBLE IN THE GRAVEL, patting the rough grey stones with my bare hand, trying to bring the world into focus with one eye closed. The trouble with losing your glasses is that you can't see without your glasses. Not well enough to find them, anyway. And certainly not on gravel. Curses. This wouldn't have happened if I hadn't been so young when I went to Moose Jaw, you know.

Actually, I haven't really lost my glasses. Just one lens — it popped out just as I was parking my car — which is why I've closed one eye. But I still can't find it. It's the same as being in the shower, when you can't tell which is the shampoo and which the conditioner. "Put a rubber band around one," a distinguished Canadian inventor told me once, when I said I was searching for a stroke of inspiration that would (a) bring relief to millions of the bespectacled (b) make me rich and (c) allow me to keep my hair clean. Where is it, anyway?

Moose Jaw was forty years ago. I was twenty-three. For reasons that had little to do with my ability, I was the newly appointed city editor of a newspaper in a city I knew little about. I looked like the office boy, or maybe the visiting grandson of our most esteemed columnist who, along with a number of other people who knew more than I did, reported to me. I decided to do something about my callow appearance. I looked up an unsuspecting optician and told him I was having trouble reading the small type on galley proofs. He aimed me at his eye chart. "E," I said, and hesitated. I walked out with a pair of horn-rims. They made me look like Clark Kent, I thought, and I could always take them off to read.

I seldom did, though from time to time in the newsroom I would push them up on my forehead, just as my grandfather used to do, except whenever he did he'd inevitably start peering myopically around the room and asking if anyone had seen where he'd put his glasses. Mostly, I just squinted away at my work, compensating for whatever distortions my Clark Kent spectacles presented. I got used to them. As the years rolled by, I got stronger and stronger lenses, wondering all the while if my eyes' natural strength and adaptability had atrophied because I'd leaned on artificial help before I needed it—just as I've managed to blame any dental problems I have not on my own careless hygiene but on the fact that when I emerged from the Labrador bush one autumn long ago, my teeth stained by a summer of iron-tainted but delicious water,

I went to a dentist on the south shore of the St. Lawrence who attacked my rusty enamel with what I'm pretty sure was a jackhammer.

Eventually, when presbyopia set in (the dreaded middle-aging of the eyes), I acquired bifocals. After a few minor adjustments — lifting my head a bit when I tried to putt (there was another good excuse, by the way), or sitting more upright at the computer so the dividing line between near and far portholes didn't come right over the line I was typing — I grew used to them, too, and it's a double-duty lens I'm groping for now, wherever it is.

I'm not good with glasses. The lovely and intelligent woman I married just after I left Moose Jaw was a pioneer of contact lenses — she wore them when you had to bathe them overnight and put them in in the morning with what looked like a tube for siphoning gasoline — taught me to clean my lenses with scalding water, so the heat would close the scratches of daily wear and tear, but since the evolution of space-age plastics, apparently you're not supposed to do that. So I just huff and puff and mop up with whatever cloth is handy, and people who work with me frequently ask how I can see through the smog. The lens that popped out in my car just now started to go its separate way after I sat on the frames while drying off from a shower one morning, my hair still gleaming with conditioner.

Hey, wait, is that it over there? No, curses, it's just a piece of cellophane. Guess I'll have to get yet another new pair, or at least a new lens. I wonder if that guy in Moose Jaw is still open.

And Who Still Shops at the Last Minute

CHAMOIS SHIRTS FROM EDDIE BAUER and cashmere scarves from J. Crew. Denim sweaters from Lands' End and golf shirts — as bright and varied in their colours as a new box of Christmas crayons — from L. L. Bean. A mohair throw from the Added Touch and, from Hedonics, where last year Gill bought me the little hand-held electronic Scrabble dictionary that settles all our arguments (and sometimes lets me cheat on the morning's cryptic crossword), a pocket — and also electronic — guide to the wines of the world: punch in the brand name and the vintage and find the region, the grape and how the bottle rates for flavour.

This was the year I decided — at last — to do my Christmas shopping early. I'd meant to for years. But every fall — and that's a lot of falls — I would put things off till the last moment. Then, as the final chords of "Silver Bells" rang out over the darkening city, I'd sprint from shop to shop, rushing in just as the storekeepers were getting ready to go home to their own eggnog, frantically grabbing one of these and one of those, loading my arms with more than I could possibly carry, stacking my car and bursting my shopping bags until, on the final stop, I could stock up on fancy paper and, later on, when everyone else had gone to bed, hold my own midnight ritual of wrapping and labelling.

Not this year, I resolved. And as early as October there I was, picking and choosing, browsing and matching. Embroidered satchels for my daughters, wooden wristwatches for my sons. For Gill, a lapis lazuli bracelet from Coldwater Creek. For her brother who has everything, a 3-D jigsaw puzzle from Lee Valley. For the kids — granddaughters or nephews — junior binoculars from the Canadian Wildlife Federation, brilliant kaleidoscopes from Lee Valley, real moccasins (they're made in Fort Smith, N.W.T.) from Winds of Change. Trinkets and treasures, gewgaws and games. And, when all was finished, wrapping paper and ribbons and bows from Regal, the granddaddy of them all.

I was shopping, of course, by catalogue. Instead of braving the crowds on the sidewalks or fighting the lineups in the malls, I was cruising the bazaars of the world without leaving my dining room table, dialling 1-800 numbers instead of circling for a parking spot, filling out printed forms instead of waiting to catch the eye of a harried clerk. I was, in short, shopping in a breeze.

And shopping, in many cases, Canadian. After Eaton's and its imitators of old, catalogues became an American phenomenon and, in recent years, many of the more astute firms have taken dead aim at Canadian customers. "Duty-free shopping," trumpets the cover of the Coldwater Creek brochure that came to my door this year, and it's not alone. But Canadian merchandisers have bounced back with a vengeance. There are nearly a thousand Canadian catalogues now, from Nova Scotia Characters (there's a hand-turned wooden bowl in there I thought about) to Beautiful British Columbia (chocolate hedgehogs, anyone?) to our own dear *Canadian Living Marketplace* and, altogether, they haul in some $2.2 billion a year. There's even a Catalogue of Canadian Catalogues.

They're fun, too (there's one called Cows — mostly folk art and cow sweatshirts — from Prince Edward Island), though so far I haven't seen anything domestic to compare to, for instance, Victoria's Secret, which I, of course, only look at for the interviews.

So there I was, as I say, pencil in hand, phone at the ready, and —

Well, I didn't do it.

Know something? I *like* last-minute Christmas shopping. I like the fuss and the frenzy and the buying on impulse; I like the carols in the streets and the crowds in the aisles, the salespeople's tips and merchants' advice; I like to *talk* to the person

I'm buying from and, when I'm in doubt, have her model a garment I'm thinking about.

I even, I confess, like the snow.

So next year, maybe. But for now, the people I'm buying gifts for won't get to read about them first.

Health Care 1: Diagnosis

I AM SITTING ON A HARD CHAIR in the X-ray wing of a very good — I am to learn — hospital. I have two gowns on: one that opens from the back, one from the front. The combination protects my modesty, I suppose, but I still feel vulnerable. They can get at me either way and stick things in me where I don't want them to. The gowns don't match; one is pale blue, the other green. I can't figure out how to tie them. My scrawny legs jut out from under their hems. My knees show. My feet are encased in floppy cotton slippers, which tie at the ankle, like mukluks, except I can't figure out how to do them up, either. My dignity is back in the changing cubicle, along with my trousers. The receptionist, young enough to date one of my sons, calls me Peter, as if I have no last name. A technician passes by without looking at me. She is in a peach pantsuit made, like my gown ensemble, of cotton. She looks sharp. Why can't I have something like that?

I'm tense and, to tell you the truth, a bit scared. I'm sure at least one of my charts will reflect what doctors call "white coat syndrome"— blood pressure that rises because someone's taking your blood pressure. Except as a visitor, hospitals — health-care facilities of any kind — are foreign turf for me. Not that I've looked after myself all these years. More, in fact, that I haven't. And now I'm getting the works. "Chest X-ray," the doctor said last week when, at last, I'd actually gone for a visit. "Blood tests, CAT scan, ultrasound, something-oscopy, barium ene —"

"Barium?" I said. "Don't they — ?"

"We'll make the arrangements," he said. "Don't worry."

Yeah, don't worry. *He* isn't sitting in borrowed jammies, in a world where strangers who call you by your first name stick things into places on your body even you haven't seen.

Emmett Hall died recently, in a nursing home in Saskatoon. He was ninety-seven. The *Globe and Mail* called him the "father of medicare," and so, on the radio, did I. At least one *Globe* reader and at least one Morningside listener wrote in to say, "Hold on, now, Mr. Justice Hall was a great man, all right, but the father of medicare was Tommy Douglas." Well, sure, if you want. Tommy Douglas was premier of Saskatchewan when the first provincial health-insurance legislation came in, in 1962, and it wasn't until 1964 that Mr. Justice Hall's report was published. But that report gave us the plan for universal, *national* health care, and that plan, amended and expanded over the years, has been one of the defining characteristics — perhaps *the* defining characteristic — of the Canada we have built. Medicare helps to make us who we are. And now, as I sit bare-legged in an unfamiliar waiting room, edgily anticipating the end of my privacy, the man who mapped it out for us is gone.

The technician in peach returns. "Peter . . . ?" she says, glancing at her clipboard. I have the impression she would *try* my last name, but the extra consonants dissuade her. An occupational hazard where she works, I guess. I realize, too, that my revery on Mr. Justice Hall has lasted perhaps five minutes at the most; I have scarcely been waiting at all. "Come with me," the technician says, and leads me down the hall.

It's not nearly as bad as I'd feared. I have been, as a doctor I know puts it, "hanging crêpe"— imagining the worst. When I actually get in to the darkness of the ultrasound room, my fears turn out to be unfounded. People are nice to me. They work quickly. They explain what they're doing. They warm the gel before spreading it on my tummy. They make me feel . . . not at home, but as if I'm being looked after, cared for. Even the barium ene . . . well, let's not talk about the barium, okay? The point is I'm in good hands.*

There's a lot of pressure on those hands these days. Everywhere, governments are wondering how much of this we can

* As you'll see in the piece that follows, those hands and their instruments, as it turned out, almost certainly saved my life.

afford. But the politicians haven't been sitting in their jammies, either, thinking of Mr. Justice Emmett Hall.

I worried about a lot of things when I was in the hospital — maybe some of them too much. But one of them wasn't money. I like it that way, don't you?

Health Care 2: Recovering

IF THERE WAS ONE MOMENT when I realized that, at last, I was going to be a butterfly again, it occurred one morning when, carefully and with a plan, I put my pants on frontwards. Oh, it wasn't *quite* the first time; some days I had been getting it right just through the laws of chance. But for a long time, my morning routine had been the same: rub the sleep from my eyes, wonder if there were still live embers in the fireplace, then reach into the heap of soft clothes at my bedside — plaid shirt, woollen socks, sweatpants — and rise to greet the day, with the northern hemisphere of my clothes headed forward, and the southern looking back on whence it came.

And now, here I was, with spring in the air, facing the world in the morning light and, well, facing the world.

These had been long, laconic, languid days. Over the winter, the medical tests that I had written about so blithely here had turned up a development that called for action: a triple A, as the doctors called it, as if it were some rare and salutary achievement, an abdominal aortic aneurysm, which looked, on the ultrasound that spotted it, like the lump I used to get on the inner tubes of my bicycle tires, except this one was in the main blood vessel running south from my heart. The solution was simple: surgery. And before I knew it, I was surfacing back to consciousness in the hands of the gentle and dedicated nurses of intensive care, with a scar down my mid-section that seemed, when I was allowed to peek, about the length of the Quebec, North Shore and Labrador Railway — although, as I knew from my own days on construction, the track across my solar plexus was infinitely better built.

The scar — and the exquisite surgical repair work that had gone on before I was stitched together — turned out to be the least of what was to affect my life over the ensuing weeks. "That's cured," said my surgeon. "Your aorta, at least the new Dacron part, will last longer than you will." But what *wasn't* cured — or not for a very long time — was my exhaustion. In fairness, the doctors (and I had an excellent team) had tried to warn me. "You're just going to feel out of things," they said. "No appetite, no energy, no desire to do anything but lie there."

"Oh, sure," I said, and went home to . . . lie down.

No warning, however eloquent, could really have prepared me. For the first couple of weeks — the larval stage, as I came to call it — I stayed in Toronto. Then, when I was up to it, a caravan of friends and family transported me to the country. They laid in a supply of easily prepared foodstuffs and easily lugged firewood ("Don't try to lift anything heavier than a phone book," the doctors said) and left me to the tranquillity they know I love.

The time at the cottage was my pupal period. Slowly, I began to test the outdoors. But mostly I just rested. My Jell-O wardrobe, as Gill called it, lay comfortably against the healing railway track of my stomach and, if my sweatpants faced the wrong way, who cared? I wasn't going anywhere. My beard grew shaggy and my muscles loose. I lost weight, as the doctors had predicted. I slept, read till my head nodded and the fire burned low, and slept again. The days dragged by.

In my lethargy, I absorbed some vital lessons: that daytime television, a stolen luxury of my working shifts, was, when I had unlimited time, even worse than I had dared to believe; that the daily news, whose every twist and turn had seemed so important, was mere background noise to my private reflections or the wisdom of the writers I was spending time with; and, most of all, how lucky I have been in the friends I've made over the years — including, may I say, the kids I have been blessed with — for the hours of my convalescence were filled with calls and letters and, on occasion, purring faxes from so many people I love but, in the whirl of everyday life, seldom have a chance to relish.

I hitched up my pants that memorable morning and resolved to try a belt buckled around my middle. As the butterfly prepared to soar again, I hoped he — I — would remember to count his blessings.

Memoirs of a Boulevardier

WHENEVER I GO TO PARIS, I like to stay at an unpretentious but comfortable and friendly hotel close to Montparnasse. All the rooms are small, by Canadian standards, but the bathrooms — and, yes, some do have bidets — are spacious and airy, and anyway, who in Paris wants to stay in his hotel room for more than a few hours of sleep? In the morning, my hotel serves delicious coffee, free, as you sit in the plush armchairs of its historic lobby and plan your day of explorations, or, if you prefer, you can stroll around the corner for hot buttery croissants from a bakery.

You can, in fact, stroll to a lot of places from my hotel: down to the river, over to Notre-Dame, to the Louvre. And, as all experienced Paris hands know, you should walk everywhere you can in Paris, for every corner is a piece of history or an architectural delight (or both), and every pedestrian or cyclist along the boulevards a lesson in fashion and *élan*, and every café an invitation to sit outdoors over a *café au lait* or a small *verre de vin blanc* while you work on the manuscript of your novel, scribbling away in the sun.

My own favourite part of the Parisian day is dinner, and my favourite restaurant is the famous Dôme, again within walking distance of my hotel. I like to have a reservation for a fashionable eight o'clock, and a trick I've learned from a Parisienne friend who hasn't smoked for years is to ask for a smoking table anyway. "In Paris," she explains, "it's the non-smokers who are the pariahs, so their section is always over by the kitchen door, while the smokers or those who are willing to suffer a little secondhand smoke get these bright places by the windows, where you can watch the promenade go by."

At the Dôme, where many literary lights have dined over the years, may I recommend the . . .

"Hey, wait a minute," I can hear you say. (You probably said it quite a few sentences ago, but I was carried away by my memories.) "Aren't you the guy who practically *brags* about never having been in Paris? Didn't you write in this very magazine, 'As I've said in a hundred speeches, in the spring of my last year at university, when all my friends were getting ready to go to London or Paris or Zagreb, I went to Moose Jaw, Saskatchewan'? And then didn't you go on to say you *still* hadn't been to Paris — unless you count the one on the Nith River in Ontario where Wayne Gretzky's grandmother used to live'?"

Well, yes, that was me. And yes, this is me, too, and now I have been there, if only for one short flying trip last autumn (the Dôme happens to be the *only* notable Paris restaurant in which I've dined, but it *is* terrific, and I hope I'll be forgiven for putting on a few airs), and even though I'll always be grateful that I've been able to see so much of Canada with the time and opportunities so many of my friends have used to go overseas, you'll never hear me brag again about having taken so long to go.

I'm sure I'd never have gone if it hadn't been for the Giller Prize, and the gracious and generous man behind it. The Giller — I hope you know this — is the $25,000 annual award for a work of Canadian fiction. It's named for Doris Giller, a literary journalist, and the man whose idea it was and who puts up all the money is Doris's widower, the real estate developer Jack Rabinovitch. The process is, in theory at least, simplicity itself. A jury of three reads — separately — all the entries (there were more than sixty this year, which made for a busy summer but was also a reminder of how much really good Canadian writing is pouring forth these days). Then they meet once, in one of their home towns, to decide on a short list of five. (Later, on the afternoon of the gala dinner at which the prize is chosen, they'll have one last meeting to pick a single winner). In 1997, the jury consisted of Bonnie Burnard, the short-story writer (she was short-listed once for the Giller Prize herself), who I always think of as a westerner but who now lives in London, Ontario; Mavis Gallant, the

Canadian author who's lived in Paris since the 1950s and who doesn't like to travel; and, ahem, me.

And now, thanks to my jury duty, I've been to Paris — you know, the one on the Seine River where Louis XIV used to live. Boy, it's hard to stop bragging. Zagreb, anyone?

A Bittersweet Graduation

HAVING AN HONORARY DEGREE from a university, someone once told me (and I agree), is like wearing silk underwear: only the person directly involved should be aware. So it's with some reluctance I write about the day I was given one of my own — a degree, that is, not a set of underwear. But what the heck, my friend and editor Bonnie Cowan has already let the sheepskin out of the bag, and the occasion was, in many ways, the happiest of my life; it's hard, maybe impossible, to keep quiet about it.

My degree took me forty-three years to acquire. I enrolled at the University of Toronto in 1952. I had, to say the least, a chequered undergraduate career. I messed up my first try, dropped out, discovered the real world to be harsh and cruel — only someone who has worked on a survey party at twenty below zero can tell you how cold it can be — and went back. What with one thing and another (the one thing being mostly working on the student newspaper), I didn't make it the second time, either. In the spring, when I ought to have been preparing for my final exams, after which all of my graduating friends set sail for London and Paris and Zagreb, I hopped a train for a job in Moose Jaw, Saskatchewan.

Four decades later, when the president of the U of T, Dr. Robert Prichard, wrote me a gracious letter asking whether, in light of some of the things that had happened to me since I left, I'd be good enough to accept an honorary doctorate of letters, I replied, in effect, "Wow! Are you kidding?" And, one summer morning, there I was, wearing, at last, my cap and gown, standing before a few hundred of my fellow graduands of 1995, all of them fanning their programs in the air to cool their excitement and their brows.

I was as excited as anyone in the hall, and, I confess, my voice shook noticeably as I spoke. "Madam Chancellor," I began, "President Prichard, honoured guests and " and here was the reason my heart was pumping "— members of our families . . ."

For there, in Row One, beside a neatly lettered sign that said simply The Gzowski Family (we pinched it later as a souvenir), were all five of my kids. Peter C. (along with his Lisa) and Alison had taken a day off from their jobs. Maria had come in from Toronto Islands. John, who keeps musicians' hours, had brushed the sleep from his eyes, and Mick (his visit was supposed to be a surprise) had come all the way from Vancouver.

It was, I realized as I beamed down from the podium, the first graduation of any sort we had shared. We're not much on ceremonies, we Gzowskis, and though there are a few (earned) degrees among my offspring, none of them ever went through the formalities of convocation. Later on the morning of my own, I wished they had; wished I'd had (or made) a chance to witness on *their* faces the pride and the tingling anticipation I saw in the eyes and the smiles of my fellow graduands — graduates, as they'd be when they stepped down — as they paraded to the platform.

But there they were, on my day, and I'm sure they could feel my happiness as I spoke.

Later — I will not bore you with my speech — we posed for some photographs. One in particular, I think — of five handsome young adults and their father, wearing a silly hat and grinning with pride in them — is the first in many years of just the six of us together.

When the ceremonies were over, I folded up my hood, my diploma and the T-shirt (GRADUATE! '95) Mick had bought for me, and my kids and I went our separate ways.

I turned on the car radio. Someone was singing the sixties song "Turn Around." The words washed over me. You know the lines I mean, about how children grow up so quickly: "Turn around and you're a young wife with babes of your own . . ." I pulled over to the curb. I wished there had been more occasions like this in our lives. I wished the kids had been up on the platform this morning and I in the audience.

I wished that, in spite of whatever achievements had led my old university to call me back after forty-three years and give me some letters to write after my name, I could do a lot of things over again.

PART THREE

Countryside

Watson Lake, White Rock, Wolfville

WHAT IT IS ABOUT TOWNS whose names begin with W that makes them special in my life I have not yet figured out. But . . . well, take Watson Lake, for example, in the Yukon. We had a golf tournament for literacy there a few years ago, and though there have been many others since in many other places, I still can't get Watson Lake out of my mind.

From the beginning, it seemed, somehow, blessed. Our plane was met at the airport by what appeared to be about half the population of the town. (Watson Lake is about 450 kilometres southeast of Whitehorse.) Our golf was played on as interesting a course as I've ever seen: nine meandering fairways carved from the wilderness by one man with a bulldozer and a fierce determination to play golf in the North. When the foursome I was in finished our round, a helicopter clattered down from the sky and whisked us up for a magic-carpet tour of the surrounding countryside — including a spectacular aerial dip into the Liard Canyon — before it dropped us back at the golf course.

That evening, at our closing banquet, there was a lovely moment.

At all our tournaments the most important prize has been the one we named for the late George Knudson. George was as great a golfer as Canada has ever produced, but our Knudson trophy had nothing to with golf. It was for, as we said, "spreading the pleasure around," which George also did, and along with the prize, thanks to one of our most generous sponsors, went two tickets to anywhere Air Canada flew. Usually, we picked the winner from the golfers and volunteers, but we'd had such a great time in Watson Lake that we couldn't choose —*everybody* seemed to have pitched in. So we gave it to the whole town, and put all the names in a hat. The winner turned out to be back in the kitchen, washing the banquet dishes, when we drew her name.

My memory of White Rock, B.C., a former summer colony on the coast just southeast of Vancouver, is poignant rather than happy. But it, too, haunts me still.

Years ago, when the program I host on CBC Radio was called This Country in the Morning, we ran a contest. The idea was to match the phrase "as American as apple pie" with a Canadian equivalent. From hundreds of entries, there was one clear winner. A young woman named Heather Scott sent me an elaborate, hand-lettered poster with the perfect solution. "As Canadian as possible," she wrote, "under the circumstances." I laughed out loud, sent her her prize and lost track of her, although, twenty years later, her poster still hangs on my office wall.

Then last year, in White Rock, I was signing books. A man of at least my own age stood quietly in line. When he reached my table, he asked me to write "under the circumstances" next to my signature.

"Are you . . . ?" I asked.

"Her father," he said. "Heather died here in White Rock last month, after a gallant battle with cancer. But your contest was important to her. It's a treasured memory."

I blinked heavily as I wrote her words. What a lovely, funny woman Heather must have been.

Then, last summer, Wolfville, Nova Scotia. Four of us drove through it last June on the way to the golf course where we'll be playing golf this summer. I fell in love: stately elms, historic architecture, a sense of belonging. As pretty a town as I've ever seen.

"Someday," I said, "I'm going to live here. There's the university [Acadia] in whose library I want to hole up and write. There's the house where I want to live. There's the restaurant [run by the partners who founded Fenton's in Toronto] where I want to eat lunch every day. And there's the sidewalk I want to stroll."

We drove on, past the signs for the Atlantic Theatre Festival, past a view of the Minas Basin, past more elms and more historic houses. My companions thought I was nuts. But I knew I'd be back. Wolfville, after all, begins with a W.

Swallow Point 1: On Passages and Places

FOR A LONG TIME, I couldn't figure out what it was that they had in common — other than, of course, that they were both weddings and that I was at them. One was in Nova Scotia, one in Toronto. One was a second time rounder, at least for the bride, and the end of singledom for a man his friends called the Teflon Bachelor; the other, a first for both — a couple whose friends couldn't imagine either with anyone else. One was in a house, with a family court judge presiding (he stayed for supper, too, having found, among other connections, that both he and the mother of the groom enjoy the racetrack); the other was in a high Anglican church with Latin on the reredos, and was consecrated by a priest who made the sign of the cross as he blessed the new couple and who led the service in a musical tenor.

There were, to be sure, some similarities. Both had, for example, moments of merriment — not counting the giggles the nephews of one of the grooms broke into when they heard, for the first time, his pair of middle names, or the smiles we all exchanged when what sounded very much like a ring went clanging across the church's tile floor just before the priest was about to call for the first exchange. In Nova Scotia, the groom, a very prosperous lawyer, appeared to hesitate for just a beat or two after "for better and for worse, for richer and . . ." as if he were thinking it over before he pledged his troth "for poorer," too. In Toronto, the groom, whose lifestyle is not one that usually calls for formal clothes, turned out, when he knelt at the altar, to have LEFT written on the sole of one of his shiny shoes and RIGHT ON on the other.

And oh, my, they were both lovely occasions, bedecked in flowers —"the arrangements were," said one of the grooms, apparently overwhelmed by the luscious displays from his aunt's garden, "very . . . *flowerful*"— marked by eloquence (well, maybe except for the "flowerful") and wit, tears of joy, moments of tenderness (a bride reaching for her handkerchief to dry her beloved's eyes as they held hands during their vows, a groom grinning as the ring, aided by a spritz of Windex, slid easily onto his beloved's finger), good cheer, good champagne and the coming together of friends and families.

But there was something else, too, something that both drew the two weddings together (they were celebrated, in fact, within a week of each other) and set them apart from other events — even, I think, other equally happy ones. And what that was became clear to me only when Gill and I, with the music of the organ and the choir and the haunting strains of the tenor solo that had filled the Toronto church still echoing in our heads, pulled into the drive of the place we share in the countryside.

Place. Just as Gill and I are rooted in the home we built together, where friends gather at New Year's, where we mark the passing of the seasons and our times — where, if I look out the window, I can see the golf course where my grandfather introduced me to his game — so, too, were the passages of two couples we care for marked by where they occurred.

The house in Nova Scotia was Swallow Point, an old and much-loved summer home on the Chester shore. Long before he had become the Teflon Bachelor, the groom had spent his childhood summers there, swimming in the waters of Mahone Bay, romping through his grandmother's garden. He and his family had come back for this most important day, and his bride and her family and friends (they came from all over the continent) instantly fit into everyone's sense of the right place for the right occasion. And the church in Toronto, too, held childhood memories for the bride. She took her first communion there and, in a life that was to take her to her own career in music, heard her first hymns from its choirs.

They all — groom and bride, bride and groom — took the first steps of their new lives in places that were already in their memories. God bless them all, and the places where they took their vows.

Swallow Point 2: A Place to Dream

THERE *ARE* SWALLOWS AT SWALLOW POINT. You see them skittering over the sun-dappled waters of the bay, mixing with the gulls and the ospreys, or swooping their laps around the garden. There are hawks, too, and thrushes and warblers — more warblers than I've ever seen anywhere — and loons that laugh in the night.

The birds, though, even the swallows, have nothing to do with the name. The point, which reaches into Mahone Bay on the south shore of Nova Scotia, is named for Jim Swallow, who settled it in the last century and who, legend has it (I've never seen him myself), still strolls the great old house, while the loons laugh under the moon.

Swallow Point is magic. I know people who have stayed there who, when they had to go into Chester for groceries, said

"Poof!" when they drove out the gate and "Poof!" when they drove back in, convinced, as they were, that the house existed only when they were in it, a kind of new-world Brigadoon.

From the lawn, standing in the shade of the sprawling weeping beech, which people drive from miles around to see, you can look over the glittering water and see, among other mirages, Oak Island, where a pirate's treasure lies. Three sides of the house are enclosed by spacious verandahs or glassed-in porches for taking the morning sun or tea in the afternoon. Indoors is dark and cool and roomy, panelled in sturdy oak, with glass-beaded chandeliers and rows of bookcases and, in almost every corner, old wooden-shafted tennis rackets and golf clubs with names instead of numbers, Monopoly games and mah-jongg sets, playthings of summers past. But sometimes, when the afternoon is quiet, you can still hear the clink of glasses from the croquet lawn and, from the garden, the laughter of pretty ladies and their dashing gentlemen friends.

From time to time, I'm lucky enough to roost there. Swallow Point — the house — was built in 1909, a summer home for one Mrs. Katherine Bailey Cooper, one of the rich Americans who were just then discovering the Chester shore. During the Second World War, the Norwegian navy acquired it as a sanctuary from the North Atlantic. Then, after the war, the Jones family of Halifax bought it — for a song in today's terms — and, though the style it was built to accommodate is now beyond their means (it's beyond the means of anybody I know, if it comes to that), the Joneses and their descendants have cherished it ever since. One of the Joneses' granddaughters, by happy circumstance for me, is Gillian Howard, who, as you'll know if you peruse this page occasionally, is the woman who shares my life.

We were there last summer. For one lovely week — lovely in that particularly gentle Nova Scotia way, when even the rain is soft — Gill and I and a small cadre of friends and family hunkered down in its airy and welcome spaces. In the mornings, the first one up would start the day's first pot of coffee and take it to the eastern porch. The next would drive out — "Poof!"— for the morning paper, more for the crossword than the news. Then toast and muffins and perhaps a shopping list, though sometimes we'd need the scratch pad for scoring the morning's Scrabble, and so on through the lazy day till we set a fire in the yawning hearth, sharing the household obligations to leave more time for Swallow Point's real purposes: conversation, the pursuit of pleasure, and time — and the space — to dream.

I, to my embarrassment, had toted along some work. It was pleasant work, to be sure, but still it was work, and at Swallow Point, surrounded by people I like, doing the things they like, I sometimes had a hard time getting down to it.

On the day before we were due to leave, we held, for the third consecutive summer, a croquet tournament. A distinguished corporate lawyer did his sweaty best to roll the lawn. The publisher of a daily newspaper went out for the makings of cucumber sandwiches and a subtly deceptive punch. Gill gathered lupines and lemon lilies from her grandmother's garden. We donned clothes as close as we could muster to white flannels and whiter shirts, hoisted the flag of Nova Scotia and broke out the mallets.

I had, I figured, about three days until my deadline. In any other setting I'd have been a mass of nerves. But this was Swallow Point. My work was not due until the publishing season of 1993. And unless my senses deceived me, that was still some decades away.

Swallow Point 3: Ladies of the House

SOMETIME WHEN MY GRANDMOTHER was in her sixties, she and my grandfather, the Colonel, bought the summer cottage at Lake Simcoe they named Betlyn, in honour of their two daughters, my aunts Beth and Jocelyn.

For the rest of her life, Betlyn was where my grandmother lived. The Colonel ran a service station in Toronto, and they kept a tiny flat there, but every year, as soon as the first buds of spring appeared, she moved north, and she stayed there till the frosts of fall, while the Colonel commuted for weekends or took an occasional well-earned week. Later, after he retired, they built a small winterized house on the same property. But Betlyn was her home, and nearly all the memories I have of her, which are many and warm, are in her role as chatelaine (if that's a word I'm allowed to use in a rival magazine) of the cottage's rambling, wood-trimmed spaces.

Whoever was there — and it often overflowed with friends and family — my grandmother was in charge. In the land around the cottage, the Colonel planted hedges, dug a horseshoe pit and built a duckwalk to the river, but inside was my grandmother's domain. She was the cook, decorator, housekeeper, shopper (on weekdays, when the Colonel and his Morris Minor were in Toronto, she would paddle a canoe into Sutton), baby-sitter, social arbiter and, as if everything else she did weren't enough, the photographer who took the pictures when other people were relaxing. "Man works from sun to sun," she used to quote with a smile, "but woman's work is never done."

These reflections came to mind last summer when, once again, Gill and I spent some time at Swallow Point. I'm in my sixties now myself (and a grandparent), and Gill and I have our own (and much-loved) country home. Betlyn, which remains in our family, is still the scene of many happy gatherings. But Swallow Point remains special, full of history and artifacts and light and shadow. It's a place that Gill's grandpar ents bought about the same time mine bought Betlyn, and a place I know played the same role in their family's history that Betlyn did — and does — in mine. It's there that my memory takes me most strongly to the summers of my youth.

Yet at Swallow Point, at least when our group takes over, there's no equivalent of my grandmother. Instead, the work —

and the responsibility — are spread around. Everyone shops, everyone cooks, everyone (when everyone feels like it) cleans up. When there's marketing to be done, whoever's going into town just asks what needs to be bought, and someone — Kevin, for instance, who runs a daily newspaper when he's not on holiday — will say, "If you get some ham and garlic and tomatoes I'll make my world-famous pasta sauce tonight," and someone else will say, "There are still enough of those lovely new potatoes for Margot's potato salad for lunch, but we need . . . " and by afternoon everything's there, and two or three people who enjoy it are in the kitchen, chopping and talking, and someone else — a different person every time — is setting the table.

There's a dishwasher, of course (a machine, not a person), so that chore's changed. But at Swallow Point even the laundry —"Anyone got any dark stuff to be washed?"— just gets done by whoever seems ready. Everyone works so everyone, more or less, can play. The old way, I imagined, had gone forever. And then one day when we were last at Swallow Point, Gill's grandmother came to call. Mamie, as the family calls her, is in her nineties now and has some trouble getting around. But she's bright and funny and proud and spunky.

Before she arrived — no one had to tell us — we tidied up. We set some chairs on one of the verandahs and sat with her for an hour or so, while she teased us all and talked of times gone by, when there were garden parties and tennis games and young sailors who came to court the girls.

And while she was there, Swallow Point felt different. It was as if time had stopped for a while — maybe, indeed, had run backward — and once again, if only for an hour, there was a lady of the house.

Swallow Point 4: The Rewards of Fame

HAVING YOUR PICTURE in *Canadian Living* every month has its drawbacks. For one, you have to watch how you behave in public, since you never know — you may remember my adventures in my local library — when some faithful reader (they're everywhere) is going to catch you doing something naughty. But it has its advantages, too, as I learned once again last summer when I was looking for, of all things, a recipe for mussels.

We were at Swallow Point, and it was my turn to get dinner. Getting, at Swallow Point, usually means doing the shopping as well as the cooking, so I thought that since I was going over to Lunenberg anyway, to visit an art gallery I know and enjoy, I could stop on the way back and pick up some fresh mussels. Cheap. And, as I remembered, easy to do. A little wine, a few onions, a garlic clove or two, some . . .

Well, maybe not that easy. Swallow Point, at least when we're there, is a competitive place. We keep track of the first three people to rise in the morning and make a triactor out of it, as at the race track. Whoever goes into town to buy fresh bagels and smoky bacon for breakfast picks up three copies of the *Globe and Mail* so the people who do the cryptic crossword can race each other. They're friendly competitions, to be sure, but they're real, as are the games of Scrabble, bridge and gin rummy that go on almost all the time we're there.

Dinner is something the same. Kevin, of the Calgary delegation, usually goes first, and sets a high standard with his pasta specialties, his Amatraciana Maltese, for example, a zesty blend of oil, onion, pancetta, tomatoes, cheese and crushed chilies. The next night, it may be Margot, with a succulent barbecued chicken, or . . . well, you get the point. It's pretty fast company, and while no one actually talks about trying to one-up the previous chef de soirée, the memory is always with you when it's your turn.

And there I was. Lunching, on my dinner day, at a Lunenberg restaurant just down the street from Houston North Gallery (which happens to be, if you're in the neighbourhood, one of the best places in all of Canada to browse for Inuit prints and sculptures as well as the folk art of Nova Scotia). The restaurant was called Magnolia's Grill, an unassuming small café, and I fell in love with its folksy charms as soon as we were in the door: snapshots on the wall, ceramic salt and peppers on the tables, menus on a blackboard. The food was even better than the ambience, and after an excellent grilled chicken salad, I dared to ask our waitress to ask the chef how she might do mussels if it were her turn to cook dinner that evening. Back, shortly, came a note: white wine, chopped garlic, celery and onion and — and here might be the special touch I sought — grated carrot. Hmm, I thought and, freshly inspired, set off for the Market at Mahone Bay — which is where, it turned out, I was rewarded for my appearances in *Canadian Living*.

"Mr. Gzowski?" said a pleasant young man on the patio. "Yes," I said. "I'm Mike Chaisson," he said. "I've wanted to get in touch with you about my vinegars." "Vinegars?" I said. "Yes," he said. "I'm a chef by training, but I've been selling specialty vinegars for about three years. In fact, wait here." Moments later, he was back from inside the market with a couple of samples from the order he'd just delivered: a basil and garlic — it looked delicious — and a blueberry and (yum) cranberry. "Try these," he said. "Hey," I said, "if you're a chef" ("I do the catering for the Lunenberg Yacht Club," he said) "then how would you cook mussels?" "Well," he said, "when you've sautéed your onions, you just take about half a cup of white wine — most people put far too much liquid in — add half that amount of the basil and garlic vinegar, then when they've steamed for a couple of minutes, pour half the liquid off, mix it with some heavy cream and reduce it for a sauce and . . ."

And, well, it worked. Spectacularly. "Best mussels I've ever had," said Kevin. "How did you — ?"

"Easy," I said. "Just drive around the Chester shore for a while until somebody recognizes you."

Sechelt: Cooking Tips from All Over

ONE OF THE MOST PLEASANT MEMORIES I carry from the Sechelt Festival of the Written Arts, on the Sunshine Coast of British Columbia, has nothing to do with literature.

It was just what we used to call at university a bull session. It started on the afternoon I arrived. After I'd been greeted at the dock and checked into my room at the festival's spacious and comfortable headquarters by some of the army of volunteers who keep everything humming, I decided to stroll over to the local wine emporium. On my way I ran into the poet Patrick Lane. We got to talking and, after making our purchases, continued our walk over to the beach, where we parked on a log. After a while, the distinguished *Globe and Mail* columnist Jeffrey Simpson came loping along from the other direction. He joined us on our log.

I can't remember (this was two or three summers ago) all of the conversation that followed, though I know we talked some baseball, that Patrick and I talked about children from previous marriages and the way the women now in our lives accepted them (the next day Patrick's wife, Lorna Crozier, gave me a beautiful poem she'd written about that from her perspective), that all of us talked about growing up in one place (in Jeff Simpson's case the United States) and trying to understand others, about landscape, about — well, sometimes just about nothing. We enjoyed ourselves and went back to the festival feeling this is the way it should be, that there should be places and times everywhere where people as disparate as a poet, a pundit and a broadcaster can spend some time just becoming friends.

The Sechelt festival is a remarkable phenomenon. It was started about ten years ago by a bright and handsome woman named Betty Keller, on a budget that would make a shoestring look like a silver necklace. A decade later, it's still chronically short of money (what in the arts these days is not?), but writers from all over the country flock there every summer, and thousands of people come to meet and hear them. And Betty Keller is still at the helm.

Betty is a writer herself. But she is also, or has learned to be over the years, a hostess, a travel agent, a counsellor, a publicity agent and, I think it's fair to say, a far more important figure in the world of Canadian writing than she realizes. And now, it turns out, she's a cookbook publisher, too. A couple of years ago, Betty and her friend Gwen Southin began asking the writers who attended the festival if they'd contribute a recipe or two to a collection that would help raise money to keep it going. They wrote to some veterans, as well.

Since virtually everyone who has been to Sechelt has had as good a time as I have, there was an enthusiastic, if eclectic, response, and the result, published this month, is *The Great Canadian Literary Cookbook.*[★]

Even though I am almost a part of the conspiracy here myself (I wrote the introduction), I should probably tell you that *The Great Canadian* etc. is not guaranteed to turn you into a master chef. Oh, there's an osso bucco from the Vancouver restaurateur (and cookbook author) Umberto Menghi that would probably impress your dinner guests (he sprinkles it with gremolata); some fancy stacked pizza from *The Best of Bridge* and, from *Company's Coming*'s Jean Paré, something called (I'm sorry) Salmon 'Chanted Evening.

But I like the more personal approaches. Maybe not Daniel Wood's method of baking a snake, which he says he got from "down under" ("First you have to get the snake down, and if you don't, you'll be under forever"). But certainly, W. P. Kinsella's bologna soup (if you make it, will they come?) and Ben Wicks' rice pudding. And maybe most of all, Robin Skelton's recipe for Celeri Ecossais: "First select previously cleaned celery sticks. Place them in a small tumbler.

[★] $15 a copy and available, I hope, everywhere. (If it isn't, just write to Betty Keller at Festival of the Written Arts, Box 2299, Sechelt, B.C. V0N 3A0.)

Now select a second glass of one-cup capacity. Place ice cubes in the glass. . . . Take a bottle of scotch whisky and fill the glass almost to the brim. Leave to mature for three minutes, then serve. Replace the celery in the refrigerator for later use."

There are also enough soup recipes to convince me, at least, that my own view of soup making as both therapy and inspiration for days at the word processor is far from unique: more than a dozen, by my count. There are stories and glimpses of stories here as well: Christie Harris's misadventures in the kitchen ("the birthday cake that went on fire"); Sandra Birdsell's childhood summer (her mother's "soup and buns" appear as delicious-sounding borscht and zwieback); Edith Iglauer Daly's American roots, which here appear in the form of an Ohio cornbread.

And memories. For me, there's even a chicken suggestion from Patrick Lane — you're supposed to splash whisky onto it, apparently — and, from Jeffrey Simpson, a cheese and noodle pie.

Do they have anything to do with literature? On second thought, you know, maybe they do.

Rankin Inlet: Scrabble Tips from the Arctic

BY THE TIME WE STARTED to play Scrabble, we had already had a drum dance, a hockey clinic, a language lesson, a reading circle, a school concert, a string-game demonstration, a birthday party, tea with the elders, dinner with the premier and a display of skeet shooting by a long-time Canadian champion, so the crowd that gathered around the board we had set up in the hotel coffee shop was small and, shall we say, jaded.

Not me, though. I'd been looking forward to this moment almost since we'd arrived, which, though it seemed longer ago, had been just a couple of days earlier.

We were in Rankin Inlet, N.W.T., a small, predominantly Inuit community on the western coast of Hudson Bay. We had come, once again — this was, in fact, our fifth annual excursion — to play golf on the Arctic ice and, as other northerners had done in previous years, the people of the town had scraped and shovelled off a course for us, this time on Rankin Inlet itself, stretching out among the nearest of the islands. (One of the hazards we'd have to cope with would be the dog-team races scheduled to finish about the same time we were supposed to tee off.)

Over the years, though, our northern tournaments — which, like all the Peter Gzowski Invitationals, are to raise money and awareness for literacy — have taken on a life of their own. By now, our golf games seem less important than the events that precede them. Our days are crammed with other activities, the best of which, it seems to me, involve a kind of cultural exchange: the northerners show us what they can of their way of life, and the people I bring along with me — different combinations every trip — share what they can of the skills and talents of their various fields.

It's always a real give-and-take. This year, for instance, our little troupe included Camilla Gryski, the Toronto children's author who has collected string games from all over the world for her books. String games have been part of the Keewatin Inuit culture as long as there's been memory, and Camilla had come to gather as well as to teach and play. Randy Gregg, the Edmonton doctor who sports four Stanley Cup rings from his days as a player, had come along only on the grounds that he could give hockey clinics, too. George Fox, the country singer, had risen bravely — and to warm applause — to try a drum dance.

And so on. The highlight this year, for me at least, had been the skeet shooting. We had borrowed a machine in Winnipeg to fire the clay pigeons into the air. Susan Nattrass, the greatest woman shooter in our history, had brought her gun from Halifax, where she's head of athletics and recreation at Saint Mary's University. And one afternoon, in the glistening sun, she had stood on the bay shore and shot soaring orange discs out of the wind. When she'd finished, some of the local youngsters had tried their hand at it, using, with Susan's coaching, the skills they'd developed hunting geese with their fathers. They'd had remarkable success. Nathaniel Kusugak, for instance, the teenage son of the Rankin Inlet children's author, Michael Kusugak, had scored a "double"—hitting, one with each barrel, a pair of discs fired simultaneously — the first time he ever held Susan's gun in his hands. Susan, in fact, had been so impressed with all the young Inuit's skills that she was trying to work out a scheme to have our borrowed machine purchased and left in the community. You couldn't help thinking, Wouldn't it be wonderful if someday there was a Canadian Olympian who'd started shooting geese on Hudson Bay?

Anyway, the Scrabble. My turn. Someone in Rankin Inlet — never underestimate the power of *Canadian Living*—had learned of my enthusiasm for the game. Before we left, they were determined that a couple of local champions get a crack at me. And now, here we were, the board spread before us. No ordinary board, either. Rankin Inlet had brought out its best: inlaid wood on a turntable, with tiles that seemed to be made of solid gold.

John Ayaruaq drew first. A J. By local custom, he chose to keep it. His brother Francis drew an S. I hit M. Threw it back. We drew the rest of our tiles and started.

Oops. John made JARRED: forty points. Francis, on his left, did almost as well. I spelled LEAVE and wondered if I should.

Still, I thought, no problem. I, after all, had been around. Then, a few plays later, John crossed his own A to make FLOATING for a fifty-point bonus, and I was, I knew, soundly beaten.

They were very good: quick, imaginative, full of all the little two- and three-letter words that separate serious Scrabblers from dilettantes, and they were playing, I was embarrassed to remind myself, in their second language.

We played again. I did a bit better. But I had met my match. We shook hands and put the golden tiles back into their velvet bag.

Ah, well, I thought, there is always the golf. But someday, I suppose, I'll have to tell you about that, too.

What's Black and Blue and Floats in St. John's Harbour? Don't Ask

A GOOD THING NOT TO DO if you're going to tell jokes on the radio, I happen to know, is to tell jokes about — and let's avoid the shorter term — Newfoundlanders. I know this because one day on Morningside we were playing around with various Canadian jokes, and up popped one with the *N* word in it. Oh, we did it with our eyes open. John Robert Columbo, the literary packrat who's put together dozens of anthologies of Canadiana, was coming in to talk about a new collection he called *666 Canadian Jokes* (there aren't quite that many in it, but John likes the title), and we'd salted the morning with examples. Most of them were pretty innocent. How many Canadians does it take to change a light bulb? (None; Canadians don't expect anyone to change.) Or what's an ig?

(A northern house without a bathroom.) But just before our Newfoundland correspondents were due to talk about something altogether different, we thought it would be amusing if we . . . and, well, it wasn't. "What's black and blue and floats in St. John's Harbour?" as they say. "A mainlander who tells . . ."

I understand this, actually. The premise of *N* jokes is that Newfoundlanders are stupid. They're not. They're funnier than most of us (I give you any one of Rex Murphy, Codco or This Hour Has 22 Minutes), they're kinder (for all their own hard times, they're the most generous province, per capita, with their donations to charity) and, if anything, wilier. John Robert Colombo, in an offering we probably should have used instead of the one we did, credits this to Silver Donald Cameron (it won a CBC competition in 1974 and 1975): A Newfoundlander is jumping up and down on a manhole cover on Yonge Street in Toronto and shouting, "Forty-two, forty-two." A passerby asks him what he's doing. Jumping on manhole covers, yelling "forty-two, forty-two" is a great sport in Corner Brook, he says; the Torontonian ought to try it. The Torontonian does — without much enthusiasm. "Put your heart into it," says the Newfoundlander. "Leap high, yell loud." The Torontonian shrugs, leaps high in the air and screams at the top of his lungs, "Forty-two, forty-two." Suddenly the Newfoundlander snatches the manhole cover away and the Torontonian disappears into the darkness. The Newfoundlander replaces the cover and starts jumping again, yelling, "Forty-three, forty-three."

Ah, jokes. My own theory is we're the funniest nation on earth, and a lot of comedy on American television, from SCTV to The Kids in the Hall to Saturday Night Live, supports it. And the difference between what's good about our humour and what's not isn't always a matter of political correctness. Could anything be more politically *in*correct, for example, than, say, Charlie Farquharson or the Royal Canadian Air Farce or — here we are again — This Hour . . .? But *N* jokes, the kind that bother people, are cruel and, except perhaps for some of our cartoonists, real Canadian humour isn't. From Stephen Leacock to Paul Hiebert's Sarah Binks to W. O. Mitchell's *Jake and the Kid* to Wayne and Shuster (from their Julius Caesar skit: "I'll have a Martinus." "Don't you mean a Martini?" "If I wanted a double I'd ask for it.") to the brightest young monologuist I know, a Quebecker-cum-Newfoundlander named Lorne Elliott, it's literate and self-deprecatory. It's whimsical ("Lord Ronald . . . flung himself on his horse and rode madly off in all directions"— a Leacock line from which, appropriately, Elliott took the title of his radio program) or political ("Knock, knock." "Who's there?" "Joe." "Joe who?" "Aw, come on, Maureen . . ."). Or it's just plain silly: An American couple are riding across the prairies by train. It's dark; they don't know where they are. The man gets out at the first stop and asks the first person he sees on the platform what town they're in. "Saskatoon, Saskatchewan," says the local. Back aboard, his wife asks the result of his quest. "I don't know," he says. "They don't even speak English here."

But it isn't cruel. It's gentle. Like us. How do you get twenty Canadians out of a swimming pool? Say, "Okay, everyone, time to get out of the pool." Or, I guess, tell them a joke that picks on people who ought not to be picked on. They'll come out all right. Fightin'.

My Country Is Not Winter. It's a Song . . .

My SEARCH for the great Canadian Song — Morningside's search really, but I developed such a profound and happy interest in it that I came to feel it was a personal quest, as well — began innocently enough one morning early this spring. A bunch of us were (surprise!) talking on the radio. Our subject was artists and money or, more accurately, artists and *lack* of money, and the singer and songwriter Sylvia Tyson was on the phone. In the opening chat, it turned out that Sylvia's bouncy and melodic hit "You Were on My Mind," which she wrote in the sixties, and which had helped to pay a lot of the mortgage on the home from which she was talking, had just been freshly recorded. "That's terrific," I said, meaning not only for her mortgage but because I had always liked the song, and later on that morning we played the original version.

What a pleasure it was to hear! You remember it, I'm sure. "Woke up this morning [beat], you were on my mind." And it started all of us thinking how many other memorable songs Canadian writers and composers had given us over the years, and to wondering which, from all the great ones, was the absolute best.

We decided to ask our listeners. To start things off we played a little medley that showed how wide the choice could be — from "Boo-Hoo" (which may not even have been written by a Canadian, come to think of it, but was one of Guy Lombardo's signature pieces) to Gilles Vigneault's haunting "*Mon Pays*," whose lyrics, even in English ("My country is not a country, it's winter . . .") still send shivers up my spine.

We had an *incredible* response. We had said from the outset that the songs people suggested didn't have to be *about* Canada (surely "Boo-Hoo" had proved that, if nothing else) or even sung by a Canadian (I don't know if anyone's ever recorded a more powerful version of "*Le Canadien Errant*" than Paul Robeson, for example); they just had to have, as the CRTC says, Canadian content. But even we — and we play Canadian music every day — had not imagined how widespread the choices would be. We had songs from long before television (did you know "K-K-K-Katie" was written by a Canadian?) and ballads from the war (or that Frank Sinatra's early theme, "I'll Never Smile Again [until I Smile with You]" was written by Ruth Lowe of Toronto?). We had jigs and reels and hymns (yes, hymns — "What a Friend We Have in Jesus," for instance, was composed in Ontario), and television themes — Don

Messer's, for one ("Got my dancin' boots on, got my Sunday best"), and Hockey Night in Canada's, which, for reasons of commercial copyright, we couldn't afford to play. (We did play the Shuffle Demons' version, though.)

We had love songs and nature songs, fishing songs and travelling songs and, from young listeners everywhere, songs right off the rock 'n' roll charts. We had "Black Flies of Ontario," and "Rise Again," from (of course) Cape Breton, and, from Saskatchewan, Connie Kaldor's haunting "Wood River." We filled the air.

Along the way, a couple of things became clear, for me at least.

One was that there never would be a single clear winner, no one song that stood by itself above all the rest. Oh, there were several that pulled remarkable numbers of nominations — the top three, if you're interested, and to give them in inverse order (like David Letterman counting down), were Ian Tyson's "Four Strong Winds" (sort of nice when you think of where the idea for our write-in had come from), Gordon Lightfoot's "Canadian Railroad Trilogy" (*three* great songs for the price of one) and, at the top, Stan Rogers' stirring "Northwest Passage."

But the other conclusion I came to was that it didn't matter. They were *all* great songs. They mattered to people. They were part of their lives. At a time when we're doing so much hand-wringing about what our culture is or whether we have one at all, maybe we should all just spend some time singing them to ourselves and to the world.

. . . Especially in Cape Breton

ALL MORNING LONG THE MUSIC of Cape Breton had been running through our heads, some of it as old as the history of European settlement, some as new as the morning paper.

"Rise and follow Charlie," Gill had warbled on our way to breakfast, and I had joined in — I, the man who never sings but who, last night, had linked arms with the organizers of the dinner and belted out "Will ye no come back again?" as if everyone else were leaving and we were staying home. "It's a working man I am," I had found myself humming over coffee, along with the tape of Rita MacNeil that filtered through the sunny dining room.

Now, a twin-engine aircraft was carrying us back to the mainland. We climbed from Port Hawkesbury, up through the wispy clouds over the Strait of Canso, heading for Halifax and a world where music plays a different role.

It had been an unforgettable trip — as pleasant and exhilarating as any of the sixty-odd excursions I've now made to play golf for literacy.

We had played a course I hadn't known before, at a resort called Dundee, on the western arm of Bras d'Or Lake. Dundee, like much of the Bras d'Or country, is beautiful. The golf course rises from the resort's main lodge up the wooded hillsides, and every fairway presents a fresh vista of land or lake. The rocky, forested islands and the sparkling water reminded Gill of Prince Rupert in B.C. and me of Algonquin Park in Ontario, and both of us of Mahone Bay, on Nova Scotia's south shore; forested, rocky islands in a glimmering setting of lake or sea is a very evocative scene of Canadian summer. Yet there was something inescapably Cape Breton about Dundee, as well: the soft light, the rise of the wooded hills, the air of peace and, always, no matter how far inland, the sense of the nearby sea.

But, as our plane headed inland, it was the music that lingered with us. All through the day before our golf, the Cape Bretoners had played music in the summer air. On the slope to the lake from the front of the lodge, the young pipers of the Gaelic College band — best in North America in their class — marched in formation, their pipes skirling over the hills. In a tent to one side, the Richmond County fiddlers, locals all, set people step dancing. On the tennis courts were songs in Gaelic, Acadian and English. The Sons of Membertou drummed a Micmac prayer; John Gracie sang some of his award-winning country songs ("She's just water under a bridge I'll never burn"); Jo-Anne Rolls performed the song that won her this year's CBC songwriting competition.

All of these performers — there were others — had been scheduled. As one organizer said, "The difficulty isn't getting people to play, it's saying no to the dozens of others who want to." But when they were finished — and when Murray McLauchlan, who had come along with us to add some mainland grace to the stage, had finished his set — there was still more to come. Onto the fairway-side stage, as the air turned brisk, strode John Allan Cameron. Accompanying him would be a host of younger Cape Breton musicians, including (to everyone's delight) John Allan's son, Stuart, and — to a roar of applause — the brilliant fiddler and step dancer Ashley MacIsaac.

On the island itself and on Broadway (he has opened for Paul Simon at Carnegie Hall), Ashley MacIsaac is a superstar, and if we were better at celebrating our own, he'd be a superstar all over Canada, too.* He's nineteen now, the son and grandson of traditional fiddlers, and a traditional fiddler himself — even when he's playing contemporary music or appearing with the Atlantic Symphony, you can hear the trill of triple bowing that gives the Cape Breton fiddle its characteristic sound. But he's unorthodox, too, his own man. He plays left-handed, holding the bow almost a hand-span from

---

* Since I wrote this, Ashley *has* become a superstar everywhere. As the kids say, excellent!

the end, and cocking his head as he sends out the lilt of his jugs and reels. He step dances while he fiddles, which for anyone less gifted would be a parlour trick but for him is an explosion of infectious energy. His music drives and soars and lifts the heart — you can't help tapping your toes. As he played in the cool of the Bras d'Or evening, with the wind rising off the lake, men near the stage lifted their arms, fists clenched in triumph — two hundred years of music given new life by a young genius. The crowd applauded steadily all through his solo, not rhythmically, not in ovation, just applause — showing their appreciation.

The golf banquet was the same. A group called Brakin' Tradition, who had played when we teed off, preceded the meal, played partway through it and, after the coffee, played enough familiar songs that all around the banquet tables red-faced old men, golfers in straw hats, pretty young waitresses, middle-aged housewives and, to my astonishment, I, were singing along.

"It's a working man I am. . . ."

Our plane began its descent into Halifax.

"It's different, isn't it?" said Murray McLauchlan, who has played and sung all over the world. "Cape Bretoners don't need an occasion to make music. They don't even need an emotion. That's just what they do when they get together. They sing. It's part of who they are. It's part of their place in the world."

Les Joix des Deux Langues

THE ONLY TIME I've ever tried to live in French was, shall we say, less than a success. It happened years ago. My young family and I were sent to live in Montreal — well, I was sent, and they decided to come with me, as Stephen Leacock said about emigrating to Canada with his parents — and I thought it would be a good idea if Dad tried to master the tongue in which, for the next year or so, he would at least presume to work. I hied myself off to Quebec City and moved in with a family in Lower Town. *Papa* was a printer. *Maman* stayed at home. They were really nice. But after we'd discussed *combien d'enfants* I had — *trois*, at the time — I'm afraid we didn't have much to talk about. Still, in a home where English didn't work, I ought to have learned how to converse with them in their language.

I didn't. I cheated. I went for long solitary walks on the historic streets, sometimes, I blush to say, settling in at a café with a stack of English magazines. I skipped meals — my wife's fears of my being spoiled by cosmopolitan French cuisine were quickly dispelled by a daily regime of roast chicken, which went into the oven in the morning and was hauled out once when *Papa* came home for *déjeuner* and again when he returned after work — in favour of movies with English subtitles and the companionship of the Château Frontenac bar. I . . . well, I missed my chance, such as it was, and returned to my unilingual ways.

I've been sorry ever since. Not so much because of my inability to communicate — I still have a smattering of the *joual* I picked up one summer on the north shore of the St. Lawrence, and enough from high school that I can decipher most headlines in *Le Devoir*— but because I believe fervently that this is a better country because it has two official languages, and think I could make the case more strongly if I could make it, with some ease, in whichever one I chose.

Oh, I know there are excesses. I think, for example, that it's silly (or worse) that it's against one law not to have French on a sign in Banff National Park and against another to have English on one in Montreal. (The whole language law of Quebec troubles me, to tell you the truth, even though I sympathize with the passion to protect French. The threat seems to me to be coming through television and music videos and down the information highway rather than popping up on the marquees of bookstores.) I think it's bizarre that, for instance, in the building where I work in Toronto there's an assumption that francophones can't find their way out the door unless the signs say *Rue Wellington* as boldly as Wellington Street, or that a hospital I know and admire has a French-language co-ordinator on the payroll but gets only five or six requests for French a year, compared with hundreds in Mandarin or Portuguese.

But if you think about them, I'd argue, not all the things we look on as nuisances are really nuisances at all. Bilingual packaging, to take the most obvious example — though I never have figured out what's wrong with having a language lesson with your morning cereal — is considered a plus in lots of the countries we export to: they think it's exotic. Is *Arrêt* on a red octagon really that hard to figure out? And as for those announcements on airplanes, as weird and unnecessary as it may seem to have someone who sounds like John Diefenbaker come on the PA to tell you *combiens de pieds* you are in the air between, say, Whitehorse and Prince George, it all becomes worthwhile when you've been out of the country for a few days and hear the first "*Veuillez boucler vos ceintures*", you know you're headed home.

And most of the bilingual aspects of our national life, surely, enrich it: the parliamentary debates; the extra channels on TV (what a shame the two solitudes don't watch more of each other's programs); the sound of our national anthem (if you're going to mangle the words in one language, why not two?); the kids in immersion courses; the very fact of our difference from so many other countries.

I suppose it's too late for me to try again in Quebec City. But I'm still glad we have two languages. Happy birthday, Canada. Or, as we say in Lower Town, *bonne fête*.

The Blasted Pine and Other Landscapes

ALTHOUGH I HAVE A FEW PIECES in my modest collection of Canadian art that I paid more for (actually, as you'll see, if I paid anything at all it was more), there is none I treasure more than my original Group of Seven. Well, maybe not quite an *original* Group of Seven, but close enough for me. It's an A. J. Casson. Mr. Casson wasn't one of the first seven members of the Group, but after Franz Johnston resigned in 1926, the other six (Franklin Carmichael, Lawren Harris, A. Y. Jackson, Arthur Lismer, J. E. H. MacDonald and Frederick Varley, if you'd like to try a little trivia on your friends) chose him as a replacement.

The work I own isn't quite an original painting, either. It is not, in fact, a painting at all. It's a . . . well, here's the story.

One morning in the early 1980s, Mr. Casson, who lived until 1992 and was a frequent and welcome guest on CBC

Radio, was sitting across from me at my messy studio table when he happened to spy the package of cigarettes I kept, in those days, at my side: Buckinghams, distinctively wrapped in red, white and gold.

"Did you know," he said, "that I designed that package?"

"Are you *kidding*?" I exclaimed.

"No," he said, and went on to recall how, as a young artist, he, like a lot of his colleagues, had supplemented his income with commercial work — including package design.

I tore off the cellophane, asked him if he'd be good enough to sign my package and, later, had it mounted in a red shadow box, which is how it hangs today on my study wall, fossilized cigarettes and all.

All of which, I hope, explains why, one day this past year, I dared to try to impress people with my knowledge of the Group's work. We had, you see, been talking about them on the radio, mostly because of the remarkable retrospective of their work that had opened at the National Gallery. People started writing with their own memories. One that caught my eye came from a woman in Vancouver, who remembered visiting, in the early 1960s, a guest house on Go Home Bay, in Georgian Bay — real Group of Seven country. Among her fellow guests was an old man whom she remembered as deaf and arthritic. One evening, a terrible thunderstorm struck. "A fireball ran around the house," she wrote. And the next morning, she discovered the old man outside, making a painting of the tree that had taken the hit.

"Sure, he's painting," said her hostess, when my

correspondent remarked on the sight. "That's A. Y. Jackson."

As I read the letter, a light went on in my head. "I wonder," I said, "if that's the famous *Blasted Pine*."

"The what?" said my colleagues at Morningside.

"*The Blasted Pine*," I said. "One of the most familiar of the Group's paintings — you know, the old tree on the rocks of Georgian Bay. Of course, I'm not sure it was Jackson who did it. But if he did, we may have here a historic document of Canadian art: a letter from someone who saw not only the storm that 'blasted' the tree, but A. Y. Jackson at work."

My colleagues searched the reference books and called the experts. No luck. No one wanted to *swear* there was no such painting — especially, perhaps, in the face of my own erudite enthusiasm — but no one could quite remember it, either. For a while, I let it pass.

A couple of weeks later, though, I happened to be in Ottawa. I leapt at a chance to see the Group of Seven show. The show was magnificent. But I almost ran from room to room looking for the work whose special history I remained convinced I knew. There were, of course, pines everywhere — jack pines, white pines, pines on islands, pines on rocks. But none, anywhere, by any artist, was called "blasted."

"*The Blasted Pine*?" said someone else I know — at last. "Oh, that's the title of a famous anthology of Canadian satire compiled by F. R. Scott and A. J. M. Smith."

"Oh, yes, of course," I said. "Maybe I could get a signed copy somewhere — and frame it."

Virtual Travel in the New World

THE AGING VOLUPTUARY FINISHES his second cup of coffee and, his crossword puzzle completed, prepares to head for work. The weather — it has been raining again — is dreary. Traffic on the parkway, as the morning disk jockey has said with his usual bad-news gusto, will be bumper-to-bumper. Tempers will fray. The Voluptuary cares not a whit. He gathers his papers and pours another coffee for the trip. "Heigh-ho, heigh-ho," he hums as his stockinged feet pad across the living room. In his study, he fires up his computer to check the e-mail — he is pleased to see the information he was seeking yesterday has arrived — and spreads his notes. He settles in. Three minutes after he has left the breakfast table, his day at the office has begun.

The Aging Voluptuary — it's been a while since we've heard from him, hasn't it?— is, as we know, not one to set a trend. He did not sit down at a computer until he was old enough to be a grandfather. His car is smarter than he is. The closest he has come to learning how to program his VCR is to stick a piece of black tape over the flashing 12:00 in the centre so it doesn't distract him. Except for the fax machine, which in his part of the countryside has become the late-twentieth-century equivalent of the party line — a source of gossip, neighbourly news and amusement — all technology intimidates him.

But he is learning. Now, as he sits at his desk, with the modem's battery of red lights blinking beside him and his laser printer purring out its first sleek pages of the day, he feels a part of his time. Home-based businesses, he has read —HBBs as they're called — are the fastest-growing segment of the economy. Already, some two million Canadians engage in some kind of domestic enterprise, and by the turn of the century, as many as three-quarters of our households will have scenes resembling the Voluptuary's morning routine. It's all part of the new age of work: leaner, "downsized" corporations, hiring people by the task rather than full time, and a generation of workers who don't expect to stick to one job all their lives. And, of course, the information revolution, the wired — or fibre-optic'd — world. All over the country, the Voluptuary knows — and sometimes talks to electronically — people who have taken their businesses home: a man who runs a national trucking company out of Chester, Nova Scotia; an important television producer who works — with her own editing suite — from her basement in suburban Vancouver; a writer here, an architect there and, everywhere you turn, consultants. By and large, they're enjoying their new lives. They feel closer to their kids, more a part of their towns and villages. They like the independence, and the freedom to set their own hours.

Their decisions to change their lives — and not all of them have been voluntary — are affecting the social landscape. If people can work where they want to, or "telecommute," as the saying goes, they don't need spaces downtown. Already in some big cities, some former office buildings are being refitted out as condos. Many small towns are feeling new life.

The Aging Voluptuary, to be sure, has not yet taken the full plunge himself. More days than not, he still goes to a workplace in the city, with its elevators and its corporate cafeteria. He still likes the companionship and the shoptalk. He realizes when he works at home that he misses office life, as, he has read, do an increasing number of people with full-time HBBs.

But his feet are wet. Much to his own astonishment, and though he no more understands it than he knows what happens when he turns the ignition of his car, he grows more comfortable with the technology every day. He has peered down the Internet. He is beginning to use his brand new CD-ROM machine as a reference shelf. He files his recipes on his hard drive and, during coffee breaks, plays bridge in an electronic foursome.

Now, in the morning silence, the fax machine whispers and beeps. "Good," says the Aging Voluptuary to no one in particular. "A message from the other world."

And Real Travels in a Very Old One

DREAM CATCHERS, which seem to have appeared in my life all over the place in the last year or so, are a lovely idea. They are, in case you haven't seen one yet — I'm pretty sure that was one dangling from the rearview mirror in the TV movie *Medicine River* — decorated, web-filled hoops, with an open circle at the centre of the webbing. Usually, they're about the size of a dinner plate, but I've seen them small enough to be worn as earrings (bought a pair, in fact, for one of my daughters), and there's one at the magical place called Wanuskewin in Saskatchewan that's almost as large as a desk.

Traditionally, the outer circle is made from bent willow and the web is fashioned of thong or sinew — you should have something natural near the centre, a feather, perhaps, or a coloured stone — but more and more people I know, not all of them Native, are making them themselves, starting with embroidery hoops, weaving the webs with thread or string and adding their own decorations: rhinestones or beads or bits of coloured glass.

You hang them, the small ones, in a window or over your bed or, more frequently, over the baby's crib. Different people have different versions of how they work. Some say simply that they keep the good dreams in and let the bad ones out. Others — this is the interpretation I prefer — say that all dreams are true when they're in your head; they only become *real* when they leave. Dream catchers let the spirits of the good dreams escape through the hole in the centre and wing their way to reality, and trap the bad ones in the web. With the first rays of the morning sun, the bad dreams evaporate.

No one seems quite sure where dream catchers originated. One of the reasons there are different ways of making them, and in fact different explanations, is that they appear in a whole range of aboriginal cultures. There's an Ojibwa legend, for instance, which I heard on Manitoulin Island, about a grandmother watching a spider spinning his web. When her grandson tries to kill the spider, she stops him. In gratitude, the spider spins a web that shines in the moonlight and teaches her the secrets of catching dreams. But a young Cree mother I know in northern Alberta who made a dream catcher for the baby she bore in the traditional way this year — a bed of boughs in a teepee — says she's never heard that story, and I've seen dream catchers as far east of Ojibwa country as Dartmouth, Nova Scotia (where I was given a particularly beautiful one last summer), and, for that matter, as far west as Vancouver Island.

How old are they? Very. My friend and neighbour Wanda Big Canoe, who's part Ojibwa and part Mohawk, told me about an archeological dig in the southwestern United States a few years ago that found evidence of them going back thirty thousand years. But Wanda, who's seen them everywhere, too, agrees their rebirth is fairly recent. It's as if, like the people who use them, they were always around, and only now we're figuring out what they mean.

They work, too. I know this not so much from experience (I'm too old to be much of a dreamer), but my granddaughters have dream catchers and . . . well, let me tell you a story.

I was in Alberta this summer, on the reserve near Calgary that used to be known as Sarcee, but which, like a growing number of aboriginal places and institutions, is now more properly called by an older name, in this case T'suu Tina. I was there — once again — for a golf tournament to raise money for literacy, but at T'suu Tina, for *aboriginal* languages and literacy. We were due to play on the Native-run Redwood Meadows course, but for several days leading up to our tournament, as had been true for most of Alberta's July, it had been raining. It was raining when I arrived in Calgary, raining when I drove out to the course and raining when I got there, with an end neither in sight nor predicted.

About an hour before we were due to tee off, I was called into the dining room. There, an elder, the chief of the local band and a young acolyte were squatted on a blanket. Tobacco burned in a pot before them. I was asked to remove any metal objects from my body — ring, spectacles, watch — and invited to join them. We smudged ourselves in the pungent smoke. The elder spoke a few words of English, then a few more in his own language. He lit a pipe. We passed it round. The praying continued, soft and solemn and (to me) mysterious.

Shortly after I left — you will have guessed this by now — the skies cleared, and we set off for our game.

Did our prayers stop the rain? I know only what I witnessed. Do dream catchers catch dreams? I only know what my granddaughters say, and that now they smile in their sleep.

Dickson Park 1: Winning the World Series

I PROBABLY HIT MY FIRST major-league home run — in the bottom of the ninth, of course, and with men on base — about 1944. It was easier then, mind you. The war had taken many of the best players overseas. The St. Louis Browns, old-timers will remember, even had a one-armed outfielder — his name was Pete Gray, and you can look this up. Still, it was the majors, and there I'd be, facing, say, Dizzy Dean, with my teammates prancing on the base paths, and I'd wait till the count was three and two and then . . .

"A home run! Gzowski — the kid from Galt — has won the game for . . ."

And I'd wake up, have a bowl of Red River Cereal and head for school.

The majors were a long way away from Galt, Ontario.

Another country, another world. But baseball was at the heart of our summers. Almost as soon as the sun melted the hockey rinks, we'd rub some Dubbin into our winter-stiff ball gloves and take to the school yards and the parks. We played scrub and work-up and flies-and-grounders and, later on, organized games, with real umpires and stuffed bases, running and throwing and laughing and hitting until the crooks of our arms were brown from the sun and each precious horsehide ball was black with tar tape.

I was a shortstop (bats R, throws R) — in real life barely good enough to make my public-school nine, but in my mind another Wiggy Wiley, the homebred hero of the Galt Terriers. The Terriers, who played in the Inter-County Baseball Association, were a motley collection of local kids — Wiggy at short and, in right field, the incomparable Moth Miller, named not only for the effortless way he darted around the outfield but for the Coke-bottle eyeglasses that made every fly he ran down an adventure — and imported used-to-bes and never-woulds.

But they were our icons. They played their games in Dickson Park, across the street from where I lived, and early on I learned to hop the fence and sneak into the shaded grandstand or lie on the sun with the other worshippers on the grassy slopes of Dickson's natural amphitheatre. Sometimes, if I hung around enough, I'd get to be the Terriers' bat boy and be allowed into the sanctum of their dressing room, with its smell of wintergreen and the clatter of spikes on the concrete floor.

And at night, I'd be called on to take a turn at short for them, and come to bat in the ninth inning with the score tied and men in base, and . . .

"It's over the fence — all the way to the railroad tracks. Gzowski, the local rookie, has won the game for . . ."

I left Galt in my early teens. Except for the occasional radio broadcast of the triple-A Toronto Maple Leafs — Joe Crysdale, who did the play-by-play, followed their away games by teletype, with a looped tape of crowd sounds chattering in the background — or the black-and-white World Series telecasts that interrupted our university autumns, baseball receded from my life, if not from my dreams.

But then, of course, the Blue Jays came to Toronto — a major-league team of our own.

I seldom went to watch them. I liked neither their original, converted football field at Exhibition Stadium nor the carpeted cavern of SkyDome. And in the early years at least, there were too many yuppies for my taste. I followed them instead on the radio, where the grass was green and no one spat tobacco juice or grabbed himself by the crotch. On radio, they smelled of wintergreen, and I listened every day.

Like all fans, I had my favourites: the graceful Tony Fernandez in his first incarnation — a shortstop, after all — and, later, the laconic John Olerud, the gentlemanly Paul Molitor. For a while, my heart belonged to the promising young outfielder Rob Ducey, who came from, of all places, Galt. But no one really caught my imagination until early in the nineties, when the sensation of the Blue Jays' farm system was a young Californian shortstop (bats R, throws R) named Eddie Zosky, whose surname, on the radio, was exactly the same as mine. Can't miss, everyone said. "Definitely ready to play for us by 1992," said Pat Gillick, the genius who built the team.

"And Zosky comes to the plate . . ."

It was not, alas, to be. The brighter the spotlight shone on Eddie, the more erratic became his play. He stayed in the minors. One account of his struggles said that when he wound up to throw to first, people in the stands moved their chairs to get out of the way. A Moth Miller of the infield, barely hitting, as they say, his weight. By 1994, even his most ardent supporters knew he'd never be a star.

Except, except. There was a moment . . .

Spring training. Florida. Late March. The Jays were in an exhibition game against the Minnesota Twins. I had them on the radio on the way home from work. Bottom of the ninth. Score tied at nine. Two men on, and . . .

"It's going . . . going . . . it's outta here. Zosky has won the game for . . ."

And you can look it up.

Dickson Park 2: Not To Mention the Stanley Cup

WINTER, WHEN I WAS A KID, began softly and gently and, if memory is correct, always well before Christmas. We would go to bed one night, warned only (there being no weather channel in those days) by the pewter grey of the evening sky and the lack of stars as it darkened, and wake — between flannel sheets if we were lucky — to a world of magic. Outside the frost-painted windows everything was white. The trees were white, as if God had spooned whipped cream over their branches; the roads were white, with only the tracks of the milkman's horse and wagon to break their drifted purity (if it was cold enough, and if we didn't fetch it quickly, the cream at the tops of the quarts of Guernsey would freeze and lift their cardboard lids); and, across the street from where we lived, the park was white as far as the eye could see.

The park — Dickson, it was called, after one of the founding families of the county — was the centre of our universe. We played tippy there in the muddy spring, baseball in the shining summer and football in the golden fall. But it was in winter that the park's life was at its richest. From the first snow, we'd ride our toboggans — that most Canadian of words, though who were we to know it?— down the slopes of its natural amphitheatre and make angels in the fields below. Snow was friendlier then, or so it seemed. We dressed for it, in scarves and toques and woollen, leather-kneed pants. It was not the enemy, as it so often seems to me now, but an element of play — the stuff of forts and missiles and, when it was mild enough, snowmen, which we'd start by packing one small nucleus, the size of a softball, and rolling it down the hill.

And then there was hockey. "The winters of my childhood," writes Roch Carrier of Ste-Justine, Quebec, in his classic Canadian story "The Hockey Sweater," "were long, long seasons." And so, in Galt, Ontario, were mine — long and cold and, as I remember them, beautiful. If Carrier's world (he is about my age) centred on three places — church, school and the hockey rink — ours centred on one, the rink. Workmen would set it up even before the first snow: a frame of pine boards, sentinels of light standards along the edges, and a shack, heated by a wood stove, in which to lace up your skates and wrap tar tape around the blade of your season's stick.

I have a hockey sweater story of my own. One Christmas, my mother, more librarian than hockey fan — the highlight of her radio week was not Foster Hewitt but Cecil B. DeMille's

Lux Radio Theatre — gave me a sweater of the style favoured by her younger and much-loved brother, who'd gone to boarding school in Upper Canada before he went away to war. My sweater was blue and white all right (as were the uniforms of my heroes, the Toronto Maple Leafs), but it was also, alas, a turtleneck, white on its torso, and blue around the waist and cuffs and itchy collar. We fixed it, or she did, in response to my lukewarm gratitude, by tacking a number on the back — an eleven, as it happened, my mother not being skilled at cutting curves — and, on the chest, a crest depicting a fierce bird of prey, which was manufactured by the textile company where my stepfather worked. It was, at last, a hockey sweater. For what team? "The Falcons," I would explain at the rink, "a great club from . . ." and before I had to come up with a city, we'd start to play.

Long or not, I loved the winters. They seemed clear, somehow, and full of dreams and promise. Sometimes, skating by myself in the cool, crisp morning light, whirring around the rink with only the scrape, scrape of my blades to break the stillness, I would hear Foster Hewitt's voice broadcasting my exploits. "The Kid has a breakaway" he would say. "One goal in overtime and the Leafs have won the Stanley Cup. The Kid shoots, he . . ."

Then, coasting back to the centre of the empty rink, I'd sing to myself from the hit parade of the day. "I'm dreaming of a white Christmas," I'd croon, the voice in my head being not my own adolescent alto but Bing Crosby's rich baritone.

And now, half a century later, when winter seems not only long but grey and miserable and more than I can bear, I'm still dreaming. It's nice, too. I hope, if the season is appropriate, it's snowing where you are.

Sure, It Rains in Prince Rupert. But . . .

THE FIRST TIME I was in Prince Rupert, about halfway up the coast of British Columbia, I saw something I had never seen anywhere else. We were on the CBC premises, finishing a training program and waiting for the weather to clear so we could get in some salmon fishing. On one side of the building, it was pouring rain, kind of Prince Rupert's trademark (though they'll be mad at me again for saying so). On the other — and the CBC building in Prince Rupert isn't much bigger than your average two-car garage — there was bright sunshine. We went out the sunny side and hit the water. A porpoise played tag with our boat. Eagles soared overhead; the ocean sparkled. We frolicked more than we fished, but on the way back into the harbour we picked up the crab traps we'd dropped on the way out, threw back the females and went ashore for a feast. The sky was still clear.

The reason I know they'll be mad at me for mentioning the rain is that another time I was on my way to Prince Rupert, to help open a new arts centre, and hoping I could cadge a plane ride over to the Queen Charlottes, I said something on the radio about needing an umbrella. They booed me when I got there — almost as loudly as people in the north used to boo me when I was host of a late-night talk show that replaced the cowboy movies on TV. But it rained that time, all right, night and day, a steady downpour that drenched a cookout we held down on the beach — I've never seen so many soggy people huddled in ponchos and determined not to give in — and soaked through everything except people's spirits.

Weather clichés, I've figured out after a lifetime of travel around Canada, are sometimes true and sometimes not. In the first years I was on national radio, I had a kind of running gag with the people of southern Alberta — chinook country. "There are no chinooks," I used to say. "There's never been one when I've been there." I stuck to my guns, through newspaper clippings, photographs, history texts, cans of "chinook air"— even an affidavit from a lady of the cloth. ("Surely you wouldn't doubt a minister. . . .") Kept it up, too, even during one visit when they painted a chinook arch on the studio window. And then one day . . . well, it's true a team of horses can be pulling a sleigh ahead of a chinook and be up to their knees in snow while the runners grate on bare ground behind them. Honest. I've seen it. You wouldn't doubt a *Canadian Living* columnist, would you?

I was in balmy Victoria in February when a cold snap hit with enough vigour to freeze the daffodils — they shattered like crystal if you ran your hand along them — and a guy I know set fire to his house trying to thaw the pipes with a blowtorch. And the hottest I've ever been in Canada was, of all places, in Tuktoyaktuk on the Beaufort Sea; I lent a hand lining the tents for Northern Games with caribou skins and began sweating so profusely my fellow-workers — the Inuit scarcely sweat at all — thought I was sick. I've been thawed out of a golf game on the ice of the Mackenzie River at Fort Providence and practically blown off my feet on the hills of Brightwood, a course in Dartmouth that overlooks the harbour. Once when I went to Churchill, it was too warm for the polar bears, and the first time I tried to "cut the devil's throat," which you do by skipping a stone into the surf at Fortress Louisburg, the water was too calm. I've flown thousands of miles in tiny bush planes over as raw and forbidding a wilderness as exists in the world, but the only times I've really been buffeted in an aircraft were once, going from Vancouver to — again — Victoria (I'm really ruining its reputation, aren't I?), when the landing was so rough the flight attendant asked to hold *my* hand, and another time on a 727 to Montreal, when we hit an air pocket deep enough to lift my Scotch and soda — not to mention my stomach — all the way to the ceiling.

Yes, there's fog in St. John's, and dry cold — and dry heat, too — on the Prairies. Yes, it rains in B.C.— never mind Prince Rupert, you should get me to tell you about Kitimat, where I was soaked every day for a Biblical forty days, and yes, there is dust on the prairie, and a gentle softness to the Maritimes. But in all my travels, I've only found one saying that's common to everywhere: "If you don't like the weather here in (FILL IN THE BLANK)," people say, "wait half an hour. It'll change."

Losing Golf Balls, Coast to Coast to Coast

ONE PICTURE OF ME I particularly treasure, or would treasure if I could remember where I've stowed it, was taken in the Yukon in, I think, 1994. I'm standing by a sign that directs the traveller to the splendid golf course at Whitehorse. The sign was carved by inmates at the local jail. It's quite elegant, except the name of the course is spelled Mountain Veiw, and the purpose of the tournament I'm about to play on its scenic and forested fairways is to raise money for Yukon literacy.

The irony of the sign, though — and I suppose all it really does is underline the importance of the tournament's cause — doesn't mean nearly as much to me as a moment in the round I went on to play. On the edge of one of Mountain View's scenic fairways, I teed up a ball and whacked it out among the soaring eagles and ravens and into the historic waters of the mighty Yukon River rolling on below. Plop. Splash. Aaahhhh.

Another time, in Riverview, New Brunswick (this time spelled correctly, as I remember), I tried to hit a similar shot into the less majestic but still very pretty Petitcodiac. Couldn't quite reach it. Lost three balls trying. Hit the Ottawa, though, on yet another occasion, standing with my friend Lorne Rubenstein, the best golf writer in Canada, beside a tee at La Chaudière in Aylmer, Quebec, and bashing balls towards the towers of the National Art Gallery across the way.

Those, and a few others, are shots I've hit into various bodies of water on purpose. Most of the time when I do it it's by . . . well, I'd like to say accident, but people who know my golf game would probably suggest ineptitude. Once I launched a beautiful arching tee-shot toward a rolling green at stately Victoria, only to watch it trickle off the edge and into the surf of the Pacific Ocean. I've hit the Atlantic from all kinds of places: from as far north as Pond Inlet on Baffin Island to as far south as Chester, Nova Scotia. And in keeping with my belief that the catchphrase should be "coast to coast *to coast*," I've also hit the Arctic Ocean from, for instance, Cambridge Bay — although, to be fair, and like Eclipse Sound off the edge of Pond Inlet, it was frozen at the time.

I've been lucky. The tournament that was first held at my home course in Ontario, the Briars (and which raised $17,000), has expanded into a network that now reaches into every province and territory. We held our hundredth event early this summer and, thanks to an army of selfless local volunteers and generous sponsors, the money we've raised for literacy is approaching $5 million. But maybe even as much as the friends I've made and the people who may have learned to read and write through our happy efforts, I've enjoyed the landscapes I've seen and the variety of golf courses I've been able to play — if, indeed, *play* is the word for what I do.

When we started, I could hit a golf ball a reasonably long distance, though I was a little wild from the tee. Over the years, I've grown significantly worse. Through age and other afflictions, I've lost about sixty yards from my drives. I can still spray them, though, and as a result I've hit balls not only into all three of our coastal oceans, but into the Assiniboine and the Red rivers, the Miramichi and the Bow, the Fraser and the Grand, three of the Great Lakes, the Bay of Fundy and the strait of Juan de Fuca. Along the way, I've also hit into marshes, ponds, swamps, sloughs, creeks, tickles and salmon streams, the prettiest of which, surely, is the one that runs across the front of the green at the spectacular Twin Rivers course in Newfoundland, where on some holes beside the eponymous rivers, fishermen wear hard hats to protect their noggins from golfers like me.

I was thinking of all this last summer. We were at the Briars. Lorne Rubenstein was making a speech. He'd been playing with me, he said, and I'd dumped my tee-shot into the pond in front of the par-three fifth hole. He went to look for it, he said. Couldn't find it. Saw instead a chirping green frog. "Pick me up," said the frog, "pick me up. If you kiss me, I'll become a beautiful princess who'll do your bidding till the day I die."

"Interested?" Lorne said he'd asked me. "Nah," I am reported to have replied. "At my age, I'd rather have a talking frog."

The Biggest Expanse of Nothing At All . . .

IN THE SPRING OF MY LAST YEAR at University of Toronto, when all my friends were getting ready to go to London or Paris or Zagreb, I — as I've said in a hundred speeches since — went to Moose Jaw, Saskatchewan. I wasn't going to graduate anyway. I'd spent my last year as editor of the student newspaper, and had forgone the pleasures of writing essays or going to lectures for those of stirring up what passed for trouble in the campus press of the 1950s, and typing and cutting and pasting into the small hours of the morning. Besides, I was out of money. *The Varsity*, which pays its editor a small salary, was coming to the end of its publishing year, and the downtown daily for which I'd been campus correspondent had fired me over an editorial I'd written in which I'd taken it to task. When a man from the Thomson chain came to Toronto seeking an affordable city editor for the Moose Jaw *Times-Herald*, I leapt at the chance. Europe could wait. I needed a job.

Although I certainly wouldn't have thought it at the time, I realize now that the train that carried me west that spring set me on a course I would follow for the rest of my working life. I've made it — barely — to Paris, once. But I still haven't been to Zagreb and my only trip to England ended in disaster. But I've seen more than my share of Canada over the years and, more or less, kept practising the craft I went to Moose Jaw to try my hand at. Much of what seeped into me there, I know now, has coloured everything I've done since.

On my way west I sat next to an Englishman, also bound for a new job, who kept his chin on his hand from the outskirts of Winnipeg until we crossed the invisible Saskatchewan border. "What do you think?" I said at last. "It's the biggest expanse of sweet nothing-at-all I've ever seen in my life," he said, though his language was a bit more colourful than that.

I quickly learned how wrong he was. Although I'd spent some short university summers in other parts of non-urban Canada — working on the power lines of Kitimat and Kildala in northern British Columbia, for example, or building a railway north from the St. Lawrence to the iron deposits of Labrador — here in the heartland I settled in. With the help of my friends at Household Finance, I bought a well broken-in Austin Healey convertible and began to prowl the endless landscape. What had looked so empty from the train became a symphony of greens and golds and browns and mauves, of field and coulee, slough and stream. In my travels — for I soon began to court a comely young woman in Regina — I felt the wrath of prairie thunder and, in its aftermath, smelled the fresh earth and heard the meadowlark sing. But I knew how harsh that land could be, as well, for the Moose Jaw of the day was still full of people who remembered the Bennett buggies of the Depression or having watched their fields blow away in the ceaseless wind, and they planted those memories in my mind.

I learned at work, too, and, though I was too young — and, I'll admit, too much of a central Canadian — to be much good at it, loved doing it. When my hours on the desk were finished, I would assign myself to stories and soon became enthralled by the raw give-and-take of Saskatchewan politics — of Ross Thatcher, having crossed the floor to run as a Liberal against his old CCF seatmate Hazen Argue in Assiniboine (I can still see Thatcher in, I think, Old Wives, cigar jutting from his mouth, growling "I've changed my mind" at the hecklers from his former party who had crowded the town hall) or of the historic debate in Mossbank between (again) Ross Thatcher and Tommy Douglas. But the real stories, I began to understand, were not of famous public figures; they were of real people, doing, as they did in Moose Jaw, real things.

I left the prairie before winter had really set in. I went to other newspapers, to *Maclean's*, to the old *Star Weekly*, to writing books, to television and to radio. I'm not through yet. But this spring, forty years almost to the week since I took that train trip, I wrap up the period that's meant the most to me: the fifteen years I've spent as host of Morningside on CBC Radio. There's been a lot of Moose Jaw in those years. And know where we're doing the last program from? Moose Jaw. It will, I know, be nice to be back.

Home

THE LIVING ROOM PINE is honeyed now, and there are dark chocolate knots on the bookshelves that frame the fireplace. The floor, also knotted, is darker still, warm and comforting, and now, you can scarcely make out the border between the original boards and the addition where the butternut table sits in the winter sun.

The table was scarred when we bought it. Someone — not us — used to sew at it, and the faint spoor of a tracing wheel is embedded in its finish. But our marks — or rather mine, for Gill is more careful — are there, too: the beginning of a bridge score on too thin a sheet of paper, doodlings from one of the many meetings we've held there over the years, the scars of crosswords.

Everywhere there are the signs of our habitation. A plywood

blue jay hangs from the beam where M. and K. strung it one New Year's, a gift to the house that has outlasted their own relationship. (M. remains convinced, wrongly, that we take it down between his visits.) Nearly every corner is hung with pictures — paintings that resonate with my travels, family snapshots, scenes that have caught our eye. But the portrait of Gill that hangs near the bedroom still lacks the glass that shattered when a Molly Maid's errant feather duster sent it crashing to the knotted floor. The kitchen counter is scorched where I put too hot a pot of stew.

Outside, too, there have been changes. Gill's garden spreads every year, though the bed she added last fall, into which she dug twenty dozen new tulip bulbs, may be her last expansion; unless we plant the driveway, there's no more room. The honeysuckle has gone from the trellis, but the towering old white pine I tried to kill by having a ditch dug past its roots miraculously still stands. The birch we planted next to it now reaches high into the thinly needled branches.

We tinker every year. Here, in the cosy den where I have written so many of these columns, bay windows now overlook the garden and, last summer, we raised the ceiling and boarded it with fresh pine. There's a storage room at the side of the porch now, where we lock away our golf clubs for the winter, and new metallic shelving in the master closet. Gill has been looking longingly at the granite slab on the kitchen island — the most utilitarian luxury we have — and wondering about the cost of replacing all the countertops, scorch mark and all. We contemplate bunks in the smaller bedroom.

But for all our fiddling, the house has been a constant in our lives. We bought it — or its antecedent — ten years ago: a small blue cottage that was, as they say, the worst (certainly the cheapest) house on the best street, the winding, hedge-lined road that runs along a southern shore of Lake Simcoe. We camped out in it that summer and dreamed our dreams. We hired an architect but found his sketches too ambitious. We gathered friends: Peter S. B., who had studied some architecture before he took up books, Libby B., the interior designer, my cousin Jack, a schoolteacher by day who has inherited all the practical skills of our grandfather. We sketched, we planned, we drew. The house —*our* house — grew on paper before Jack signed on the Finnish craftsmen who were to build it. A windowed clerestorey (PSB's idea) would give the illusion of space. Sliding glass doors — Jack insisted — opened onto a cedar deck. Libby had us keep the space free and open, and added touches of modest — and practical — elegance: the efficient, brass-bound fireplace; the granite on the island; the food-processor on a hinged shelf that swings into action when it's needed. You can cook here, and talk to your guests.

We moved in the next spring — not full-time, for both our jobs require us to sleep in Toronto much of the week, but every moment we could get away. It worked for us from the outset. It's been home.

I pause now, and look at the new pine on the ceiling. In the years ahead, it, too, will turn to honey. I can wait. A person has a lot of addresses over a lifetime. If he's lucky, he'll end up where he belongs.